FRENCH IMPRESSIONISM
AND ITS ORIGINS

LIGHTING UP THE LANDSCAPE

This exhibition has been sponsored by
GUINNESS PLC

FRENCH IMPRESSIONISM
AND ITS ORIGINS

LIGHTING UP THE LANDSCAPE

National Gallery of Scotland

1 August – 19 October 1986

National Galleries of Scotland, Edinburgh

Contents

Foreword   7

Acknowledgements   9

Impressionism and its Origins   11

Maps   22-3

Catalogue

The Salon   27

The Sketch   37

Barbizon and mid-century Landscape   49

Prelude to Impressionism   61

Impressionism   71

Artists' Biographies   81

Bibliography   87

List of Lenders   90

Photographic Credits   91

Foreword

Lighting up the Landscape continues the policy we have adopted in recent years at the National Gallery of organising our exhibitions around a particular picture or group of pictures in the permanent collection. In providing a context for our paintings we have tried to enrich our visitors' understanding and appreciation of them by showing that they belong to an historical process, and that the form they take can be partly explained by what has gone before and what contemporary artists were doing at the same time.

The star of this year's show is Camille Pissarro's *The Banks of the Marne at Chennevières*, a masterpiece of his pre-Impressionist style and one of the great French landscapes of the period. The exhibition provides us with a splendid opportunity to reassess the influence on the young Impressionists of such illustrious predecessors as Corot, Courbet, Delacroix and Rousseau; but also to bring to the visitor's attention many less familiar artists who have been unjustly overlooked. By a happy coincidence 1986 is the centenary of the Edinburgh International Exhibition of Industry, Science and Art. The fine art section of this ambitious enterprise included a loan exhibition of 19th-century Dutch and French pictures, drawn mainly from Scottish collections. It is indicative of the taste of that time that no Impressionist works were included. The preference then was for the darker, more traditional landscapes of the Barbizon School painters, such as Théodore Rousseau, whose *Edge of the Forest of Clairbois, Fontainebleau* was shown in 1886 and is included here. Taste has changed and in our time it is, of course, the Impressionists who everybody wants to see. We hope to redress the balance and to offer visitors to our exhibition the best of both worlds.

The exhibition has been organised by Michael Clarke, Assistant Keeper at the National Gallery, who has received guidance throughout from the Keeper, Hugh Macandrew.

I would like to thank all our lenders, both private individuals and public institutions, who have so kindly allowed us to borrow their pictures. Guinness PLC have given us most generous and much needed financial support for which we are deeply grateful.

Finally, it is appropriate at a time when we are drawing attention to our own Impressionist collection to remember with gratitude those generous benefactors who contributed so much to its formation: Sir Alexander Maitland; Sir John Richmond and his niece Mrs Traill; and Mrs Kessler.

TIMOTHY CLIFFORD
Director

7

Acknowledgements

I am very much aware of the support and assistance I have received from many individuals in the preparation of this exhibition. Dr Richard Verdi initially suggested the subject and Richard Thomson has generously shared his knowledge with a novice in the field. Jack Baer, Timothy Bathurst, Desmond Corcoran and S. Martin Summers have all been most generous of their time in securing loans from private owners. I would also like to thank, for their help in different ways, Anne-Marie Bergeret-Gourbin, Dr Richard Brettell, the Cowling family, François Delestre, Lucy Dew, Dr Peter Galassi, John Gere, Dr Gerhard Gerkens, Professor Francis Haskell, Professor R. L. Herbert, Christopher Lloyd, Jane Munro, Dr Nicholas Penny, Pierre Rosenberg, David Scrase, John Sillevis, Robert Stoppenbach, Bernard Terlay and Ian Wardropper. In the National Gallery Hugh Macandrew has given sound advice, Janis Adams has supervised the catalogue through its various stages and it has been efficiently typed by Sheila Scott, Julie Murphy kindly assisted in the preparation of the artists' biographies and John Dick has specially cleaned our Pissarro of Pontoise and the beautiful early Corot.

MICHAEL CLARKE

Impressionism and Its Origins

The inspiration and focal point of this exhibition is the National Gallery's painting *The Banks of the Marne at Chennevières* (no. 12) by Camille Pissarro which was most probably exhibited in the 1865 Salon. A brief examination of the picture's qualities explains why it met with such official approval. It is a large painting which commands attention. The composition is carefully ordered and the diagonal recession of the river Marne creates a sense of space and perspective that is easily and clearly understood. The colours are quite dark and subdued and there is nothing to startle the eye. It was painted in the studio and not out-of-doors and was the result of careful preparation based on a number of drawings and oil-sketches made by Pissarro of this part of the Marne.[1]

The *Marne at Chennevières* is not a painting one would readily associate with an Impressionist painter, whereas Pissarro's beautiful *Kitchen Garden at L'Hermitage, Pontoise* (no. 102), also in the National Gallery, fulfils many of one's expectations of an Impressionist landscape. It was painted in 1874, the year of the First Impressionist exhibition, and is quite a small picture, unsuited to a grand exhibition hall. It lacks the formal structure of the Marne picture and was painted out-of-doors, in front of the scenery it portrays. The colours are bright and, on close examination, quite surprising. The Impressionists relied not so much on tone or local colour to model their pictures, as on the 'warm' or 'cool' properties which cause colours of even the same tonal value to advance or recede in relation to one another, thus creating illusions of depth and volume. The brightness of a painting could be heightened by juxtaposing colours that contrasted strongly with one another. The Impressionists eschewed tradition and used modern oil-paints in which poppy oil, which was creamier in texture, had superseded linseed oil as the binding medium. It retained the mark of the brush-stroke and it was also slower to dry, allowing more 'wet-in-wet' reworking of the paint on the canvas. The Impressionists also favoured white or pastel-coloured grounds which gave a light key to their paintings. The ground of the *Kitchen Garden at Pontoise* is clearly visible as a light pink and is deliberately left unpainted in some areas to provide the highlights in the picture.

In his Pontoise landscape Pissarro has captured a rural scene at a precise moment in time without making any concessions to the niceties of formal balance or highly finished brushwork. The atmosphere of an autumn day is conjured up in a manner that would appear to owe little to the pictorial conventions found in the earlier, more traditional painting of the Marne.

If one looks again at the two paintings, however, it is possible to discern features which challenge the conventional wisdom that one of them is still relatively 'old-fashioned', whilst the other is more 'modern'. The brushwork in the Marne picture is broader and heavier than that found in the Pontoise painting, but it is also quite broken and does not wholly conform to the academic requirement of a smooth finish. The use of the palette knife in the application of paint is clearly evident and this is a technique Pissarro learnt from the Realist painter Courbet, who had flouted convention both in his art and in his life. If the subject-matter of Pissarro's two pictures is compared, then that of the Marne can be argued to be the more unusual of the two, for within the broad framework of this river scene are two strikingly contemporary details – a small mill or factory and a boating-party. The Pontoise picture, on the other hand, shows a rural scene unaffected by progress and a class of subject with a long tradition in French art. So whilst it is generally correct to say the Pontoise picture is more modern than that of the

Marne there are inconsistencies in such a judgement. Equally, although Impressionism, especially in its technique, did represent a break with the art of the past, it can also be shown to have had important links with what had gone before.

This exhibition is about the early landscapes of the young Impressionists, in particular Monet and Pissarro, and seeks to place them in the broader context of French 19th-century landscape painting. It concentrates on the years leading up to the exhibition held by the *Société Anonyme des artistes, peintres, sculpteurs, graveurs...* which opened on 15 April 1874 at the Parisian studios of the photographer Nadar and is generally referred to as the First Impressionist exhibition. This is a title that art history has subsequently conferred upon this event, for the participating artists did not then call themselves Impressionists and, due to considerable disagreement within their ranks, settled on a rather bland title for their corporate identity. It was not until their third exhibition, in 1877, that the *Société* agreed to the adjective Impressionist, and this decision was doubtless influenced by the fact that many critics had already used the word in connection with their paintings. The French word *impression*, from which 'Impressionist' is derived, is a difficult one to define. It gained widespread critical use in France in the course of the 19th century, and was usually taken to mean a rapid, fleeting and ultimately insubstantial visual perception of an object or objects. It was quoted in connection with the 1874 exhibition in both complimentary and derogatory ways – the most famous example of the latter being the satirical review by Louis Leroy which appeared in the journal *Le Charivari* in which one of the protagonists exclaims of Monet's *Impression: Sunrise* (fig. 1) '*Impression* – I was certain of it. I was just telling myself that, since I was impressed, there had to be some impression in it ... and what freedom, what ease of workmanship! Wallpaper in its

Fig. 1. Claude Monet, *Impression: Sunrise* 1873, Musée Marmottan, Paris.

embryonic state is more finished than that seascape'.[2] The speaker was a landscape painter of the old school.

Impressionism, with its emphasis on a new kind of visual response to nature, seemed to challenge both the rules of the governing body of French art in the 19th century, the Ecole des Beaux-Arts, and the traditional conventions of landscape painting. Landscape was a category which had never fitted easily into academic theories of art. In 19th-century France it rose from being a genre that was considered of no great importance and greatly inferior to history painting, to one that enjoyed wide popularity. Some, though by no means all, of the artists who contributed to this process of change can be cited as important precursors of the Impressionist landscape.

The most consistently successful landscape painter in France in the first half of the 19th century was Camille Corot, whose long career stretched from the 1820s, when the historical, academic landscape held sway, through to 1875. On many occasions Corot painted out-of-doors and used bright colours in his works – as the Impressionists did – but he is never described as an Impressionist. This would be to remove him from his historical context and it would also constitute an oversimplification of the facts. Furthermore, although the young Impressionists (particularly Pissarro and Sisley) were undoubtedly influenced by Corot's paintings, the older master remained devoted to the Salon, and he discouraged Cézanne's friend Antoine Guillemet from participating in the First Impressionist exhibition, 'My dear Antoine, you have done very well to escape from that gang.'[3]

The variety found in Corot's pictures reflects the complexity of the various types of landscape that evolved in the 19th century in France. The first of these was the 'historical landscape'. This was an academic type of landscape which was based on the works of 17th-century artists, above all Nicolas Poussin, but also Claude Lorrain and Gaspard Dughet. It depicted an idealised, Italianate scenery in which the composition was carefully and artificially arranged. It is illustrated in this exhibition by a painting by Dunouy (no. 1). It received official sanction in 1817 with the institution of the Rome Prize for Historical Landscape at the Ecole des Beaux-Arts.[4] There was already the Rome Prize for Painting (history painting) which was awarded annually and the winners completed their studies at the French Academy in Rome. It was decided to hold the competition for the landscape prize every four years and, whilst this clearly denoted landscape to be an inferior category to history painting, it still accorded it a rank above portraiture, genre or still-life. The first winner of the prize was Achille-Etna Michallon, who had studied under Bertin and Valenciennes and would be, for a short time, the teacher of Corot who, in turn, encouraged some of the young Impressionists and their contemporaries. These personal links between succeeding, and very different, generations of landscape painters should not be overlooked.

The principles of the historical landscape had been set out by the landscape painter Pierre-Henri de Valenciennes in his treatise *Elémens de Perspective Pratique* published in 1800. His ideas were elaborated further by his pupil, J. B. Deperthes, whose *Théorie du Paysage* appeared in 1818. Deperthes defined the historical style in landscape as: 'The art of composing scenery from a selection of the most beautiful and the most noble that nature produces, and of introducing into it persons whose actions, whether they recall an historical act or present an imaginary subject, are able to arouse the keenest interest of the spectator, to inspire his noblest feelings or give wings to his imagination'.[5] Baudelaire would later scornfully describe this class of landscape as 'ethics applied to nature'.[6]

The relationship between these treatises and the Impressionists is a distant but subtle one. Whilst much of their art represented the culmination of a process of reaction against the ideas put forward by Valenciennes, the unfinished appearance of the Impressionists' paintings had much in common with the academic notion of the landscape sketch (*étude*) made out-   13 of-doors. These open-air sketches functioned as visual notes, to be referred to in the studio when composing the final picture. Valenciennes advised they should be executed quickly and warned against those artists who, 'fall into grave error by wishing to give excessive finish to their studies which should only be rough sketches [*maquettes*] made in haste, to capture Nature exactly'.[7] Whether Valenciennes's advice was followed to the letter is unclear. Of the many landscape sketches that survive, a considerable number would appear to have been finished in the studio (no. 19), whilst others were partly imaginative (no. 16) and not direct transcriptions of nature. Their qualities, though, were those of empirical observation and spontaneity in execution – qualities that would reappear in Impressionism. Lest it be thought that Valenciennes's treatise was totally ignored by later generations, it should be pointed out that it was read by the Impressionist Armand Guillaumin and recommended by Camille Pissarro to his son Lucien.[8]

It is often forgotten that, in the earlier stages of their careers, the Impressionists executed preparatory sketches for their paintings. A number of compositional sketches (*esquisses*) by Pissarro survive (nos. 10, 39), as does a pair of *études* made near Montpellier by Bazille (nos. 41a and b), an artist who was a close friend of Monet but was tragically killed during the Franco-Prussian War. Bazille and Monet worked together in the Forest of Fontainebleau to the south-east of Paris in 1865. The main reason for Monet's visit was to undertake preparatory studies for a life-size painting of a picnic in the Forest, the *Déjeuner sur l'Herbe*, which he intended to submit to the 1866 Salon in emulation of Manet's celebrated *Déjeuner* which had been shown at the Salon des Refusés in 1863. Monet's painting was to be based on studies made in the open air, and his models for the picnickers were drawn from his immediate circle, including his mistress Camille and Bazille. The painting measured 15 x 20 feet but was never completed and was later cut down. Two fragments survive today.[9] There was also a 4 x 6 feet *esquisse*, now in the Pushkin Museum in Moscow.[10] In an *étude* (fig. 2) loosely related to the *Déjeuner* Monet executed a woodland study (*sous-bois*) in the Forest which is strongly reminiscent of Corot both in composition and in the slightly dainty treatment of the foliage.[11]

Fig. 2. Claude Monet,
A Forest Road ca. 1865,
Private Collection.

In the works of their maturity the Impressionists dispensed with the traditional distinction between a sketch and a finished picture by combining the qualities of both.

The historical landscape was generally considered to have become out-moded by the middle of the century, although the Rome Prize was not discontinued until 1863. There was another type of landscape mentioned in the treatises, however, and this was the rural style of landscape (*le style champêtre*). Valenciennes and earlier writers such as Roger de Piles had deemed it inferior to historical landscape. Deperthes differed from his predecessors, however, by pleading equality between the two categories. He defined rural landscape as: 'In a word, to represent faithfully an expanse of country with the part of the sky which dominates it, and seen in the light that falls on it at the very moment when the painter sets out to capture its appearance'.[12] Whilst this definition might be thought to anticipate the Impressionist landscape, it was actually derived from the works of the 17th-century Dutch masters such as Jacob van Ruisdael whose paintings were well represented in Parisian collections. In the early 19th century in France rural landscape found its most consistent exponent in Georges Michel, whose dramatic panoramic views were heavily indebted to Dutch art – Michel's assimilation of which must have been aided considerably by his employment at the Louvre as a restorer of Netherlandish painting.

Dutch landscapes undoubtedly provided a major source of inspiration for those French artists who, from about 1840 onwards, worked in the Forest of Fontainebleau (Valenciennes had actually suggested the Forest as a possible substitute for the Roman countryside as an area for artists to sketch in). They are now known as the artists of the Barbizon School after the village of that name situated on the edge of the Forest whose magnificent oaks, heaths, rocks and pools were seen as comparable to those found in the paintings of Ruisdael, Hobbema and the other Dutch masters. Barbizon was the best-known of the many localities which attracted communities of artists working away from Paris. Others included, to the north of Paris, that in the L'Isle-Adam/Valmondois area; to the south in Arceuil, Sceaux and the valley of the Bièvre; to the west round the Sèvres factory, Bois de Meudon and the Ile de Séguin. This last area was frequented by historical landscape painters in the early years of the century and, due to the presence of the Sèvres porcelain factory there, continued to attract artists who were employed in the factory, including the landscape and animal painter Troyon who enjoyed great success in mid-century. With the expansion of Paris, whose population more than doubled to over one million between 1810 and 1847, artists moved further west along the Seine, beyond the Sèvres area, to small towns such as Bougival and Louveciennes, and it was there that Pissarro and Sisley would work in the 1860s and 70s.

The most distinctive and controversial of the Barbizon artists was Théodore Rousseau, whose dramatic forest scenes were excluded, between 1836 and 1847, from the Salon. Many observers correctly viewed this as an injustice and Rousseau was often referred to as '*Le Grand Refusé*'. The historical landscapist Bidauld, a member of the Salon jury, was singled out for particular vilification by contemporaries and later writers. Lanöe and Brice, in their history of French painting published in 1901, recalled of Bidauld that he had been, 'the implacable enemy of the young generation and had contributed more than anyone to hindering the emancipation of the Romantic School'.[13] This exclusion of a new and vital movement in art was a phenomenon that would be repeated in the difficulties faced by the young Impressionists and their associates in their attempts to gain regular admission to the Salons in the later 1860s.

Rousseau's landscapes were described by his contemporaries as 'romantic'. The fundamental point about the romantic approach to landscape painting was that it encouraged a personal response to nature – landscape should inspire emotion and sentiment in the viewer. Natural disasters, dramatic seascapes, picturesque ruins, decaying forests – these were the landscapes of Romanticism. Rousseau's 'romantic' *The Forest in Winter at Sunset* (fig. 3)[14] was 15

Fig. 3. Théodore Rousseau, *The Forest in Winter at Sunset* 1845-6,
Metropolitan Museum of Art, New York, Gift of P. A. B. Widener, 1911.

begun in the winter of 1845-6 and was based on the recollection of a deep wood in Bas-Bréau in the Forest of Fontainebleau. The intricate network of living and dead timber is imbued with suggestions of decay, the passing of time and of melancholy.

The critic who most strikingly defined the doctrine of Romanticism and its effects on French painting was Charles Baudelaire. In the section of his 1846 Salon devoted to landscape he wrote, 'There is one man who, more than all of these, even more than the celebrated absentees, seems to me to fulfil the conditions of beauty in landscape ... You will have guessed already that I am referring to M. Rousseau – ... Like Delacroix, he adds much of his soul to the mixture; he is a naturalist, ceaselessly swept towards the ideal'.[15]

A comparison of Rousseau's forest scenes with those executed by the Impressionists reveals a fundamental difference in technique, however. Bazille's *Landscape at Chailly* (no. 61) an early Impressionist picture painted in the Forest of Fontainebleau in 1865, shows the woodland made famous by the Barbizon School painters, but painted in much brighter colours. In Bazille's painting light plays over the greenery of the Forest, it does not filter out mysteriously from dark woodland glades as it does in the works of Rousseau, Diaz and their associates.

It was the great achievement of Rousseau and his contemporaries to push landscape to the forefront of French artistic life. By the 1850s the strength of French landscape painting was widely recognised. This was a period, too, when the traditional categories of painting – history, genre, rural life – were becoming increasingly intermingled. Thus Claude Vignon observed of Jules Breton's celebrated *The Gleaners* (no. 5), exhibited in 1855, that it was classed as a landscape, 'although it could just as willingly be returned to the series of paintings of everyday life; but it is the characteristic of this new school [of painting] to trouble itself much less about the categories into which the classical school wishes to enclose specialities, for nature is always mixing them together and that is what makes up life'.[16] This mixing of categories would be taken by the Impressionists to the point where their work defies classification in such conventional terms.

There was no single movement that can be said to have directly preceded Impressionism. Instead, Monet, Pissarro and their friends studied and adapted from the art of individual artists such as Corot, Daubigny, Courbet, Boudin and Jongkind.

Corot's influence is in some ways the most difficult of any to evaluate. Equally at home in the historical or the rural style, he also excelled in the landscape sketch. Pissarro proudly listed himself as Corot's pupil in the early 1860s and Monet is known to have admired him greatly. From the 1850s, however, Corot had practised in his exhibition pictures a very personal type of landscape painting which, in its gentle air of unreality, could best be compared with that of the 17th-century artist Claude Lorrain. It was a poetic landscape produced mainly in the studio and with little reference to open-air sketching. His late style is illustrated in his *Souvenir des environs du Lac de Nemi* (no. 13) which was exhibited at the Salon in 1865. Critical reaction to this painting was somewhat jaded and was generally of the opinion that Corot's paintings differed little from one another, and that the mists in which the scenery was enveloped could equally derive from Italy or from the banks of the Seine. Such works were devoid of reference to the contemporary landscape and in spirit harked back to the historical landscape. And yet a number of works by the young Impressionists testify to the profound effect Corot had on their formative years. The Impressionists ignored Corot's late style and concentrated on his fresher, earlier work. Corot was also an encouraging and undogmatic teacher, admitting to Pissarro that whereas he saw pictures in terms of tones he quite understood the younger artist's wish to paint in pure colours.

The landscapes of Daubigny were possibly of more immediate relevance to the Impressionists. His career developed steadily despite his early failure to win the Rome Prize for landscape in 1837. A change in Daubigny's art was noticed by his friend, the writer and painter Frédéric Henriet, who published an article on him in *L'Artiste* for 1857 in which he listed the three prime qualities of Daubigny's paintings – sincerity, a faithfulness to the feelings or sentiments of nature; a limpid clarity achieved by a new luminosity: improvisation visible in the direct sketch, the *impression*.[17] It was also in 1857 that Daubigny launched his *botin*, his floating studio from which he depicted the rivers of France (particularly the Oise) both in paintings and in a collection of prints published under the title *Voyage en bateau*. Monet would also use a floating studio, in emulation of Daubigny. In a number of his landscapes of the 1860s and 70s Daubigny either anticipates or follows closely behind the young Impressionists. Thus his London river scenes of 1866 (no. 72) have a sense of movement and atmosphere that points forward to Monet's Dutch riverscapes of 1871, whilst his orchard scenes of 1873 (no. 82) probably benefitted from his knowledge of the heightened colours of Impressionism.

The third artist who clearly influenced the young Impressionists was Gustave Courbet, not so much by his choice of subject-matter, as by his anti-authoritarian manner and his style of painting with dark, heavy colours, often applied with the palette knife. Pissarro's Salon paintings of the 1860s (nos. 9, 12) and Monet's dramatic marines (no. 73) provide evidence of a Courbet-inspired phase in early Impressionism.

In an *Interview* published in 1900 Monet recalled that the education of his 'eye' – the very quality in Monet admired by Cézanne – had been begun by Boudin and completed by the Dutch painter Jongkind.[18] Monet was referring to his early years as a painter in the 1850s and 60s in his native Le Havre on the Normandy coast when he was instructed in the art of painting out-of-doors by these two older artists. The art of Boudin, in particular, provided Monet's introduction to the tradition of the open-air sketch, the aesthetics of which he increasingly came to believe should form the basis for all his pictures.

Pissarro's early work is best located in the tradition of pastoral landscape painting that had developed in the 1850s. The life of the pastoral painter was described by Henriet in his book *Le Paysagiste aux Champs* of 1876.[19] The book does not mention any of the Impressionists, instead discussion is of the Barbizon painters, Corot, Daubigny, Chintreuil, Français and a host of lesser names. Henriet also lists the areas they worked in and where, he claimed, they remained free of the polluting influence of the city.

When the young Impressionists' paintings first appeared in the Paris exhibitions they were comparatively well received. Pissarro's landscapes at the Salon des Refusés in 1863 received encouragement from Castagnary, a staunch admirer of Courbet. He advised Pissarro to develop further, 'Not finding his name [Pissarro's] in the preceding livret [Salon handbook] I suppose that he is a young man. The manner of Corot would seem to please him: a good master, sir, but one must above all beware of imitation.'[20]

Pissarro exhibited at both the 1864 and 1865 Salons (nos. 9, 12) and it was to the latter that Monet successfully sent two seascapes, one of which, *The Mouth of the Seine at Honfleur* (fig. 4)[21] was chosen for illustration in the souvenir album *L'Autographe au Salon*. It was praised

Fig. 4. Claude Monet, *The Mouth of the Seine at Honfleur* 1865, The Norton Simon Foundation, California.

by the pseudonymous critic 'Pigalle' as, 'the most original and supple seascape, the most strongly and harmoniously painted to be exhibited in a long time', possessing, 'a somewhat dull tone, as in Courbet's; but what richness and what simplicity of view! M. Monet, unknown yesterday, has at the very start made a reputation by this picture alone'.[22] In his successful depiction of the blustery weather and vibrant luminosity of the Seine estuary Monet was elaborating on the achievements of Boudin.

1865 also saw the most concerted effort by Monet and his friends to assimilate the art of the masters of Barbizon by working in the open air in the Forest of Fontainebleau. Monet and Bazille had first painted in the Forest during the Easter holidays in 1863. On their second visit in 1865 they stayed, as before, in the small village of Chailly-en-Bière. Renoir and Sisley were also working in the Forest, staying in the village of Marlotte some miles to the south-east of Chailly. Whereas the Barbizon painters adopted a rural life-style, wearing peasant smocks to paint in and living in picturesque cottages in or near Barbizon, the Impressionists, particularly Monet, were more city-orientated and remained very much visitors to the Forest.

Monet was undoubtedly the most progressive of the young Impressionists. His 1867 series of three views of Paris from the Louvre, of which one is included in this exhibition (no. 84), are almost photographic in the way in which they 'freeze the action' on the busy streets below the palace. Buildings, people, sky and water are defined not by line and tone but are seen as areas of coloured light.

The modernity of the Impressionists found its literary counterpart in the writings of Emile Zola who became the self-proclaimed spokesman for the young artists. He equated the Impressionists' portrayal of contemporary landscape and townscape with his concern in his own novels to describe modern life in a precise, objective manner. He wished to sweep away old conventions; thus Rousseau and Millet were considered to have, 'lost their steadiness of hand and the excellence of their eyes';[23] whilst, 'If M. Corot would agree to kill off once and for all the nymphs with which he populates his woods and to replace them with peasant women, I would like him beyond measure.'[24] Zola forcefully declared his preference for Corot's open-air sketches rather than his studio pictures and roundly castigated Daubigny for producing too many commercial pot-boilers. The new heroes were the Impressionists. Monet was highly praised, and of Pissarro's *Banks of the Marne in Winter*, exhibited at the 1866 Salon, Zola wrote, 'You are a great blunderer, sir – you are an artist that I like.'[25] These forthright views outraged most of Zola's readers and must have damaged, by association with their author, the reputations of the artists they praised. Zola was equally uncompromising in his articles on the 1868 Salon. The past was once again rejected: 'Classical landscape is dead, killed by life and truth. Nobody would dare to say today that nature needs to be idolised, that skies and expanses of water are vulgar and that it is necessary to represent harmonious and correct horizons if one wishes to produce beautiful works'.[26] According to Zola, progress in landscape painting was being hindered by the countless number of more conventional painters whose works filled the Salons every year and lacked any individual interpretation of nature. In contrast, Pissarro's landscapes were, 'supremely personal and supremely true' and bore no resemblance to any others. This was only partially correct, for Pissarro's landscapes still betrayed debts to Courbet and Daubigny, but Zola was always capable of suppressing or ignoring ideas which did not suit his line of argument. He categorised Pissarro as a *naturaliste* ('creator of skies and fields') and Monet as an *actualiste*[27] – presumably meaning he painted the topical and the contemporary: 'As a true Parisian he [Monet] brings Paris to the countryside, he is unable to paint a landscape without placing in it ladies and gentlemen who are all dressed-up. Nature would seem to lose its interest for him if it were not to bear the mark of our manners and customs.'

1867 was not a successful year for the Impressionists at the Salon. Bazille, Cézanne, Monet, Pissarro, Renoir and Sisley were all rejected and a number of them signed a petition for a new Salon des Refusés. Whilst the following years brought acceptances for some of them, particularly through the efforts of Daubigny, the seeds of secession from the Salon had already been sown.

The Franco-Prussian War of 1870-1 resulted in Monet and Pissarro moving to London and caused Bazille's death. It may be that the physical and mental disruption which the war brought about enabled the Impressionists to break finally with past landscape traditions. In the early 1870s, after the war had ended, it is possible to discern a new balance in their paintings, which are also smaller in scale, thereby indicating they no longer wished to produce the grand Salon piece. Their joint investigations of colour and light produced a unified style with which they examined their chosen environment which was mainly the suburbs and outlying towns of Paris. Monet was at Argenteuil from 1871 to 1878, Pissarro at Pontoise (for a second time) from 1872 to 1882, and Sisley at Louveciennes from 1870 to 1875.

The 1872 Salon, which many hoped would encourage renewed faith in French art, was generally considered to be a disappointment, though it was agreed that the best section was that devoted to landscapes. Many of the critics felt that the time had come for an alternative major exhibition in Paris, so the 1874 exhibition of the *Société Anonyme*, the so-called First Impressionist exhibition, would have come as little surprise to most of them and many reviewers praised its existence, if not its contents. The artists who participated in this first venture were of a much wider variety than is often suspected. Apart from the Impressionists, there were such now forgotten figures as Attendu, Brandon, Debras, Levert and Léon-Auguste Ottin.[28] It has recently been discovered that this first exhibition received many more favourable reviews than has hitherto been supposed.[29] However, the apparent spontaneity of execution and unresolved quality of many of the Impressionists' works troubled most writers. Reference has already been made to Leroy's infamous satirical article which attacked, in particular, Monet's *Impression: Sunrise*, and 'Marc de Montifaud' (Marie-Amelie Chartroule) was equally severe, considering it to have been, 'executed by the infantile hand of a school child who is spreading out colours on any sort of surface for the first time'.[30]

It was not until 1876 that a piece of critical writing appeared which comprehended fully the technical advances the Impressionists had made in their paintings. Edmond Duranty's *The New Painting: Concerning the Group of Artists Exhibiting at the Durand-Ruel Galleries* was published around the time of the Second Impressionist exhibition.[31] Although he did not name him, the artist Duranty praised most was, by implication, Degas, whose work was essentially figurative. Duranty discussed landscape frequently in his essay, however, and his most extended passage on the subject demonstrates his grasp of the optical qualities of the 'New Painting' as opposed to the darker tones he found in the works of the Romantics:

And yet everyone has crossed 75 miles of countryside in summer, and seen how the hillsides, meadows, and fields disappear, as it were, into a single luminous reflection which they share with the sky. For such is the law that engenders light in nature – in addition to the particular blue, green or composite ray of light each substance absorbs, it reflects both the spectrum of all light – rays and the tint of the vault that curves above the earth. Morever, for the first time painters understand and reproduce these phenomena, or try to. In certain canvases you feel the vibration and palpitation of light and heat. You feel an intoxication of light which is something of no merit or importance for those painters trained outside of nature and in opposition to it. It is something much too bright and distinct, much too crude and explicit.[32]

The mention of the unity of sky and ground recalls advice given by Valenciennes to begin a sketch with the sky which sets the tone for the rest of the picture, but phrases like 'the vibration and palpitation of light and heat' can only be applied to Impressionist paintings such as, appropriately, Pissarro's *Kitchen Garden at Pontoise* and other landscapes of 1874 with which we end our exhibition.

MICHAEL CLARKE

Notes to *Impressionism and Its Origins*

1. For example, Brettell and Lloyd no. 64 recto.
2. Translated and reprinted in Nochlin pp. 10-14.
3. Recollection by Monet, 1905, quoted by Rewald p. 316; but see Tucker in Moffett p. 116 n. 68 who questions the accuracy of Monet's statement.
4. See Grunchec, 1983 and 1984/5.
5. Deperthes p. 210.
6. Baudelaire p. 104.
7. Valenciennes p. 404.
8. Boime p. 136.
9. Musée d'Orsay, Paris and Private Collection; Wildenstein nos. 63a), 63b).
10. Pushkin Museum, Moscow; Wildenstein no. 62.
11. Private Collection Wildenstein no. 58.
12. Deperthes p. 144.
13. Lanöe and Brice p. 86.
14. Metropolitan Museum of Art, New York; Sterling and Salinger pp. 84-6.
15. Baudelaire pp. 108-9.
16. Vignon p. 249.
17. Herbert, 1962 pp. 47-8.
18. Translated and reprinted in Nochlin pp. 36-45.
19. F. Henriet, *Le Paysagiste aux Champs*, Paris, 1876, see Brettell.
20. Castagnary, pp. 175-6.
21. Norton Simon Foundation, Pasadena; Wildenstein no. 51.
22. Quoted in Rewald p. 123.
23. Zola p. 72.
24. Ibid. p. 73.
25. Ibid. p. 74.
26. Ibid. p. 115.
27. Ibid. p. 111.
28. On the First Impressionist exhibition see Tucker in Moffett pp. 93-117.
29. Tucker, 1984.
30. *L'Artiste*, 1 May 1874, pp. 308-9.
31. Translated and reprinted in Moffett pp. 37-49.
32. Moffett p. 43.

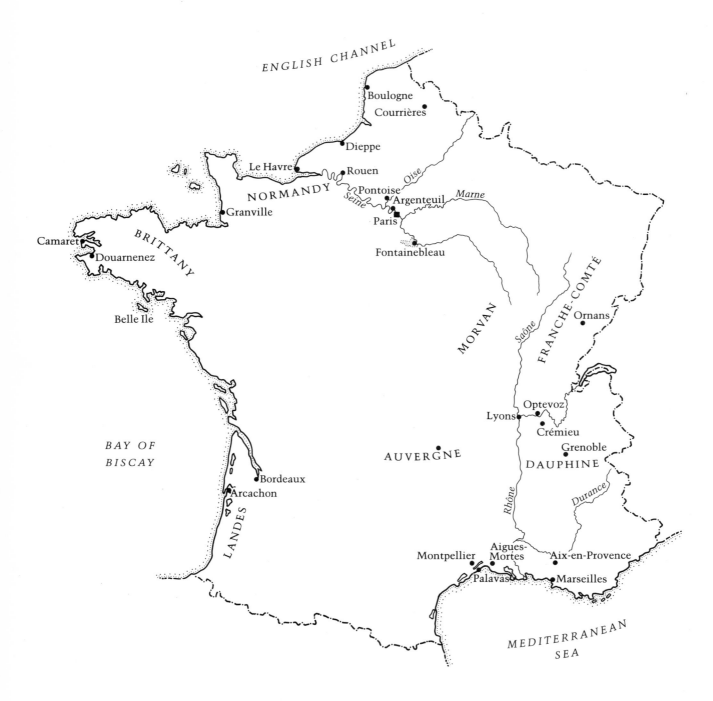

ENGLISH CHANNEL

Boulogne
Courrières

Dieppe

Le Havre • Rouen
NORMANDY
Pontoise
Oise
Seine   Argenteuil   Marne
Granville
Paris

BRITTANY   Fontainebleau

Camaret
Douarnenez

MORVAN   FRANCHE-COMTÉ

Belle Ile   Ornans

Saône

Optevoz
Lyons
Crémieu
BAY OF   AUVERGNE   Grenoble
BISCAY   DAUPHINE

Bordeaux
Arcachon
Rhône   Durance
LANDES

Montpellier   Aigues-
Mortes   Aix-en-Provence
Palavas   Marseilles

MEDITERRANEAN
SEA

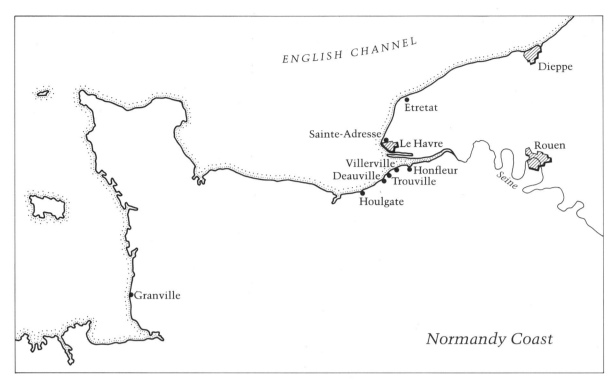

Normandy Coast

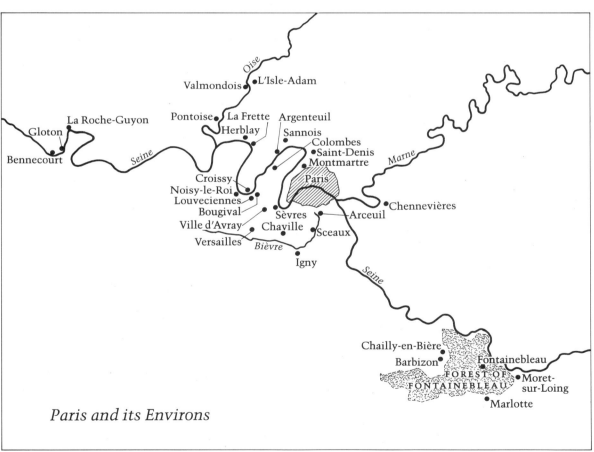

Paris and its Environs

The Catalogue

Catalogue entries are arranged chronologically within each section.
Measurements are in centimetres, height precedes width.
* Denotes paintings reproduced in colour.

The Salon

This section of the exhibition sets two early Salon pictures by Pissarro in the context of a selection of Salon and other related 19th-century landscapes. Landscapes painted for the Salon, including those submitted by the young Impressionists, were often large and carefully composed. They were intended to attract the attention of visitors in the enormous exhibition halls of the Palais de l'Industrie. The fresh and informal approach to landscape which the Impressionists evolved increasingly conflicted with the demands of such official 'exhibition' art. The Paris Salons were the major art exhibitions in France and were usually held annually. Artists eagerly sought inclusion in them where their paintings would be seen by enormous crowds, discussed in numerous reviews and, it was hoped, be purchased by the government or by private collectors. The Salon was a symbol of government support for the arts and, like governments, was subject to change. It was originally administered by the French Royal Academy then, from 1793, by the Fine Arts Division of the Institute of France and finally, in 1863, control passed to the Ministry of Public Education. Its location also changed. At the beginning of the 19th century it was situated in the Louvre, then the Tuileries, on one occasion it was in the set depot of the Opéra, and it eventually was given a regular venue in the Palais de l'Industrie. The jury system of judging the works of art submitted to the Salons also changed many times. In 1848 the Revolutionary government abolished the jury system altogether but it was later reinstated. The famous Salon des Refusés (refused works) of 1863, which included Manet's *Déjeuner sur l'Herbe*, was but one manifestation of frequent dissatisfaction with the decisions of the juries. Perhaps the most remarkable fact about the Salon was that it continued unchallenged for so long. The Royal Academy exhibitions in London had many rivals by the 1850s, but it was only in the later decades of the 19th century that the Salon was faced with a similar degree of competition, including that provided by the First Impressionist exhibition in 1874. The Salon was originally intended to celebrate 'high art' (mostly history and religious painting) but, in the course of the 19th century, the lower genres of painting, including landscape, gained increasing prominence.

[1]

[2]

ALEXANDRE-HYACINTH DUNOUY

[1] View of Sora

Canvas: 138 x 198.5
Signed and dated, lower right: *A. Dunouy f. Romae 1789*

This classical landscape was possibly exhibited in the 1791 Salon as *Vue d'Italie, Paysage, Chute d'eau, orné de figures et d'animaux*. The view is of the small town of Isola de Liri to the south-west of Sora in central Italy. Dunouy exhibited further views of Sora at the Salon in 1822 and 1824. The subject was also depicted many times and from the same viewpoint by Bidauld, including the major early work he exhibited at the Salon in 1793; *Vue de l'Ile de Sora dans le Royaume de Naples*.[1]

Private Collection

1. Musée du Louvre, Paris; Gutwirth, 1978 no. 29.

JEAN-BAPTISTE-CAMILLE COROT

[2] View in the Campagna ('La Cervara')

Canvas: 69.5 x 95
Signed, lower right: *Corot*
Lit: Robaut no. 200[1]; Rosenberg, 1974 no. 23.

This has traditionally been described as the picture exhibited by Corot at the 1831 Salon as *La Cervara campagne de Rome*; it is more probably the *Campagne de Rome* which was shown at the 1827 Salon and thought by Robaut to have been lost.[2] Its compositional oil-sketch is in the Louvre and is dated 1827.[3] It would therefore have been submitted to the Salon by Corot during his first visit to Italy 1825-8. The scenery does not correspond to that found near the little village of Cervara (now called Cervara di Roma) which is about 45 miles east of Rome in the Sabine Hills.[4] Apart from an obvious debt to Gaspard Dughet, the dramatic lighting and the ox-cart in this picture also show the influence of Dutch art on Corot. He never wholly renounced the classical landscape, but his exhibition pictures (except for his late idealised landscapes) give more evidence of direct study of nature than those of most of his contemporaries.

Kunsthaus, Zürich

1. According to whom the signature on no. 2 was added later by Corot at the request of his nephew Lemaistre.
2. Suggested by Toussaint, 1975 pp. 21-2.
3. Robaut no. 2459, offered by Corot during his first stay in Italy to the painter Barbot.
4. A. and R. Jullien, 1984 pp. 188-91, they point out that the landscape in no. 2 is possibly closer to that of the quarries of Cervara just north of Rome.

PIERRE-ETIENNE-THEODORE ROUSSEAU

[3] The Edge of the Forest of Clairbois, Fontainebleau

Canvas: 65.4 x 104
Signed, lower left: *TH. Rousseau*
Lit: Green no. 27.

Between 1836 and 1847 Rousseau's landscapes were excluded from the Salon earning him the title '*Le Grand Refusé*'. This painting was possibly the *Edge of the Forest* (103 x 130 including frame) that was turned down by the jury of the 1839 Salon.[1] Although he had received a relatively orthodox training, Rousseau made no concessions to classical landscape, concentrating instead on producing what Fromentin later termed 'a modern form of Dutch art in France'.[2] His landscapes were based, in particular, on the Forest of Fontainebleau south of Paris, an area he knew from the late 1820s and where he settled in the late 1840s. The *Forest of Clairbois* was neither sold nor exhibited in his lifetime but fetched 13,600 francs in 1870 and 33,500 francs in 1873.[3] Rousseau's paintings commanded very high prices up to the First World War, as did those of Corot and Millet; after which Impressionist prices rose sharply. This landscape was exhibited one hundred years ago in Edinburgh in the 1886 *International Exhibition: French and Dutch Loan Collections*. This exhibition provided a representative indication of British taste of the time which was dominated by a fondness for the works of the painters of Barbizon and of the Hague School. Unfortunately, much of the foreground of no. 3 has darkened irretrievably since it was painted. Something of the freshness of colour Rousseau was able to achieve can be ascertained from the sketches by him in this exhibition.

Glasgow Museum and Art Gallery

1. Suggested by Green p. 52.
2. Fromentin p. 276.
3. Edwards sale, Paris, 7 March 1870; Laurent-Richard sale, Paris 7 April 1873 no. 47, both quoted by Green.

JEAN-ALEXIS ACHARD

[*4] Landscape near Grenoble

Canvas: 131 x 211
Signed, lower right: *J. Achard*
Lit: Huault-Nesme no. 20.

This was exhibited at the Salon in 1845 where Achard was awarded a second-class medal. It is a formal celebration of the Dauphiné in south-east France, Achard's adopted region of which he was the foremost painter in the mid-19th century. The formula he adopted for such pictures was a mixture of classical composition (derived from the work of Claude Lorrain)[1] and topographical observation (the scenery here represented shows the valley of Gresivaudan dominated by the rocks of Saint-Pancrasse and La Dent de Crolles). It was about this time in his career that the colours he used became brighter, the shadows more transparent. He was described in the 1864 Salon by Amedée Cantaloube as, 'At the head of the new landscape painters ... His little canvases shine like precious stones',[2] whilst in 1866 Jules Castagnary wrote of 'the great army of landscape painters' then invading France in which Achard was placed at the head of the 'first corps of the Army of Paris'. The only Impressionists Castagnary included were Monet as a 'second lieutenant' and Pissarro as a 'captain'.[3] Achard was one of the many now largely forgotten landscape painters whose work was placed (including this canvas for a while) in the Luxembourg, the 19th-century museum for the greatest living French artists.[4] Achard also had personal links with a number of younger, more progressive artists. In 1846 he became the teacher of Harpignies (nos. 37, 38) and in 1858 and 1859 was at the Saint-Siméon Farm, near Honfleur (no. 55), where he was sketched by Boudin seated at a table in the company of Jongkind, Emile Van Marcke and Monet.[5] A visitor to Saint-Siméon in 1865, recorded seeing pictures by Achard decorating the rooms there.[6]

Musée du Louvre, Paris

1. Achard copied paintings by Claude in the Grenoble Museum and the arrangement of the foreground in no. 4, especially the diagonals created by the paths and the stream, may have been derived from Claude's *Pastoral Landscape* (Roethlisberger no. 79) at Grenoble.
2. Quoted by Huault-Nesme p. 18 no. 46.
3. Castagnary (1869) pp. 3-4.
4. See Toussaint, 1974. Other landscapists represented in the Luxembourg included d'Aligny, Breton, Corot, Daubigny and Harpignies.
5. Huault-Nesme, p. 16 no. 41.
6. Delvau.

JULES BRETON

[5] The Gleaners

Canvas: 92.7 x 137.8
Signed and dated, lower left: *Jules Breton 1854*
Lit: Thompson, J. no. 7; Weisberg 1981/2 no. 50.

The Gleaners brought Breton the first of many official awards he would receive during his career, a third-class medal, when it was exhibited at the Universal Exhibition in 1855. The scene is set in the late afternoon near the village of Courrières in Breton's native Artois in the north-east of France. Gleaning, the gathering of the corn left after the harvest, was an activity granted to the poor of the community on a charitable basis. Breton's picture avoids many of the hard realities of rural life. Normally, gleaning was only allowed at the end of the day when the harvest was completely over, yet here the harvest is still in progress. The women and children are well-fed and attractive[1] and the field-keeper on the right is merely picturesque. Millet treated the same subject more severely in his *Gleaners* of 1857,[2] but to less critical acclaim and his picture remained unsold for seven years, whereas Breton's found a ready purchaser. The content of Breton's paintings, and of *The Gleaners* in particular,

has been subjected to much recent analysis,[3] but their visual qualities have been somewhat ignored. In his exhibition pictures Breton followed standard academic practice by executing a number of preparatory sketches, many of which were painted out-of-doors.[4] The attractive, bright colouring of these filtered through to finished pictures such as *The Gleaners* in which the high colouring of much of the landscape looks forward to Impressionism, which Breton later described as an art of excess.

The National Gallery of Ireland, Dublin

1. The model for the girl in profile in the right foreground was Elodie de Vigne, whom Breton married in 1858.
2. Musée du Louvre, Paris, see Herbert, 1976 no. 41 and a comparison of the two paintings by Bezucha in Weisberg, 1982 pp. 1-13.
3. See Sturges.
4. The two surviving studies for figures in *The Gleaners* are nos. 50A and B in Weisberg 1981/2; a good selection of Breton's sketches is included in Sturges nos. 53-71.

EUGENE ISABEY

[*6] View of Granville

Canvas: 119 x 175
Signed and dated, lower right: *E. Isabey./1855*
Lit: Miquel, 1980 X no. 1325.

This romantic view of Granville on the Normandy coast was exhibited by Isabey at the Universal Exhibition in 1855 (as *Vue prise à Granville*[1]) where his works attracted great critical attention. The most favourable reviews were those by Du Camp, who did not specifically discuss the Granville picture, and by Gautier: 'The *Vue prise à Granville* shows that M. Isabey is incontestably our best marine painter and does landscape as well as anyone.' Isabey's rapid, free manner of painting appealed greatly to Gautier: 'We lay great stress on this quality of M. Isabey's because it is tending to become uncommon; nowadays a different manner has prevailed, and people try as much as possible to make the brushwork disappear under a meticulous finish; we like this free and honest manner where the human touch is evident over the reproduction of things.'[2] This stress on a work of art conveying the individual touch and temperament of its creator was a central tenet of Romanticism. Although the Impressionists developed a much more objective, less anecdotal manner of representation than Isabey's, their opposition to 'meticulous finish' in their work shows some affinity with Romanticism.

Stoppenbach and Delestre Limited

1. Acquired 1892 by John J. Johnson, 1912 presented to the Philadelphia Museum of Art, de-accessioned 1947.
2. *Les Beaux-Arts en Europe* 1855, quoted by Miquel, 1980 IX p. 135.

[5]

[7]

EUGENE BOUDIN

[7] Pardon of Sainte-Anne-la-Palud, Gulf of Douarnenez (Finistère)

Canvas: 78 x 155
Signed and dated, lower right: *Eugène Boudin 1858* and lower left: *E. BOUDIN 1858*
Lit: Schmit no. 185; Philadelphia no. VI-9.

This was Boudin's first submission to the Salon where it was exhibited in 1859 and described by Baudelaire as 'a very good and careful painting'.[1] Boudin himself expressed considerable dissatisfaction with the work, the result of many preparatory studies, 'There is too much in it, yet nothing that would specifically characterise Brittany; the colour and light are lacking in something'.[2] Boudin's disappointment in not recreating the 'atmosphere' of the place was perhaps an expression of frustration at the compromises he had had to make for an official 'finished' painting. His oil-sketches and pastel studies were already very different ('improvised in front of the sea and sky'[3] as Baudelaire described the pastels) and undoubtedly influenced the young Monet whom Boudin met for the first time in 1858. In portraying a 'pardon' (a mystical, penitential pilgrimage) Boudin had chosen a traditional subject that took place in an area that would become especially popular with painters in the later 19th century.[4] He himself had witnessed this 'pardon' in 1857. The 'pardon', seen by 19th-century visitors to Brittany as characterising the intense Catholicism of the Bretons, was a mixture of the religious and the secular.[5] Church ceremonies were followed by wrestling bouts, dancing and other fairground activities and these could last for three or four days. The style of some of Boudin's drawings for this painting is reminiscent of 17th-century artists such as Jan van Goyen; the organisation of the composition is generally indebted to earlier Dutch market and fairground scenes. The women wear the *coiffes* or headdresses of Porzay, Quimper and Pont-l'Abbé, whilst the men have their traditional coats and wide-brimmed hats. The effect is picturesque and discursive, very different from the powerful symbolism and disquieting composition of Gauguin's later Breton masterpiece *The Vision after the Sermon* (National Gallery of Scotland).

Musée des Beaux-Arts 'André Malraux', Le Havre

1. Baudelaire p. 199.
2. Notebook, 25 January 1859, Jean-Aubry p. 24.
3. Ibid.
4. On artists in Brittany see Jacobs, chapter three, who points out it was American, not French, artists who really discovered and colonised that region.
5. Weisberg, 1980.

[8]

4. Jean-Alexis Achard, *Landscape near Grenoble*

6. Eugène Isabey, *View of Granville*

9. Camille Pissarro, *'The Towpath'*

14. Louis-Alexandre Dubourg, *Sea Bathing at Honfleur*

PAUL HUET

[8] The Cliffs at Houlgate

Canvas: 157 x 227
Signed, lower right: *Paul Huet*
Lit: Minneapolis no. 49.

This large and dramatic work was exhibited at the Salon in 1863, purchased by the State and allocated to Bordeaux on the recommendation of Dauzats.[1] It can be considered a late survivor of the romantic landscape. Baudelaire referred to Huet in 1859 as, '*a veteran of the old guard!* (I can apply this familiar and grandiloquent expression to the debris of a fighting glory like *Romanticism*, which is already so far behind us.).'[2] Houlgate, where Huet sketched frequently 1856-62,[3] is just a few miles west of Deauville and Trouville on the Normandy coast, an area where Boudin was already executing his pre-Impressionist studies of sea and sky. A comparison of the stark contrast of lighting in the sky in Huet's painting with that in Monet's *Seascape, Shipping by Moonlight* in this exhibition (no. 73) shows that the younger artist must certainly have looked at romantic landscapes. Huet was strongly influenced throughout his career by English landscape painting and the mood of this pictue, in which a drowned body is carried up the beach, is reminiscent of Turner. Huet's small oil-sketch for this composition shows the influence of Constable in its colouring and has a different arrangement of figures on the beach.[4]

Musée des Beaux-Arts, Bordeaux

1. Miquel, 1962 p. 213, who also states Delacroix admired the work and suggested alterations.
2. Baudelaire p. 198.
3. Miquel, 1962 p. 206.
4. *Normandy Coastal Scene* Kunsthalle, Bremen; Gerkens and Heiderich p. 143.

CAMILLE PISSARRO

[*9] 'The Towpath'

Canvas: 81.9 x 107.9
Signed and dated, lower right: *C. Pissarro. 1864*
Lit: Lloyd, 1980/1 no. 3.

This was almost certainly exhibited at the 1864 Salon, either as *Bords de la Marne* or, less likely, as *La Route de Cachalas à la Roche-Guyon*. The terrain does not correspond with that near La Roche-Guyon, but if it is of the Marne then its present title must be incorrect, as the Marne, according to a contemporary account, did not have towpaths.[1] Pissarro still described himself as a pupil of Corot at this stage of his career and the colours, lighting and manner of painting the trees are all reminiscent of Corot's work. The subject of river scenery was probably inspired by Daubigny who frequently exhibited subjects of this type at the Salon.

Pissarro's sketch for this painting is no. 10 in this exhibition.

Glasgow Museum and Art Gallery

1. La Bedollière and Rousset, pp. 2-3 described the Marne as 'spared from towpaths'. The path in no. 9 is also too far away from the river to have served as a towpath.

[10] Sketch for 'The Towpath'

Canvas: 24.4 x 32.5
Signed, lower right: *C. Pissarro*
Lit: Lloyd, 1980/1 no. 2.

Pissarro was following academic practice in executing this compositional sketch for '*The Towpath*' (no. 9). In the Salon picture, however, he preserved many of the rough, blocked-in qualities of the sketch and made few concessions to the fine, meticulous finish expected in an exhibition picture. Impressionism dispensed with such stages by combining them in one picture and bringing the freedom of the sketch to the finished picture. Many similar oil-sketches were probably lost when Pissarro's studio at Louveciennes was occupied by enemy troops during the Franco-Prussian War 1870-1.

The Syndics of the Fitzwilliam Museum, Cambridge

GUSTAVE COURBET

[11] Ornans Landscape

Canvas: 86.4 x 129.5
Signed and dated, lower left: *64 Gustave Courbet*
Lit: Fernier no. 376[1]; Bowness and Toussaint no. 77.

Courbet spent most of 1864 in his native Ornans which is in the Franche-Comté, close to the Swiss border. Courbet's handling of paint and the range of colours he used influenced Pissarro's large Salon landscapes around this time (nos. 9, 12). Courbet's rough, *sauvage*, manner of applying paint thickly with the palette knife was a direct challenge to the smooth finish of most pictures accepted at the Salon. This painting was purchased on 21 July 1865 by the English collector John Bowes from a M. Basset[2] who may have been acting as an intermediary between Bowes and Courbet.

The Bowes Museum, Barnard Castle, County Durham

1. See Fernier no. 611, a weak repetition, dated 1867, of the general landscape of no. 11.
2. Possibly the M. Basset mentioned by the American dealer George Lucas, 27 February 1873 'At Bassets, 7 rue Mausant', Randall II p. 374.

[10]

[11]

CAMILLE PISSARRO

[*12] The Banks of the Marne at Chennevières

Canvas: 91 x 145.5
Signed, lower right: *C. Pissarro*
Lit: Pissarro and Venturi p. 20; Thompson, C., pp. 18-19; Lloyd 1980/1 no. 4.

This was almost certainly exhibited at the Salon in 1865 as *Chennevières au bord de la Marne*. In style and format it should be compared with the Glasgow *Towpath* 1864 (no. 9) and the Chicago *Banks of the Marne in winter* 1866.[1] All are large, ambitious, formal compositions which, in their bold use of paint, owe a great debt to Courbet,[2] though the colour and tonal ranges are wider and remind one that Pissarro studied with Corot. In the Salon catalogues of 1864 and 1865 Pissarro listed himself as a pupil of Anton Melbye (1818-1875) and Corot. The subject and diagonal composition recall the numerous river scenes painted by Daubigny on the banks of the Marne, Oise and Seine.[3] The pastoral calm of Daubigny's river scenes inspired the photographer Ildefonse Rousset to publish in 1865 *The Tour of the Marne*, with text by Emile de la Bedollière, in which that river is described as, 'a charming river, sprinkled with islands whose vegetation rivals that of the tropics, bordered with laughing villas, and dominated by coasts with a view stretching over an immense horizon...'[4] La Bedollière continued by attributing to the banks of the Marne, 'the aspect of a virgin nature', but Pissarro has chosen not to emphasise such intense rural escapism; instead we see a boating party on the river and, to the right, a small mill or factory. These contemporary details, deliberately chosen, are, however, easily assimilated in the grand, almost classical, design of the painting. Pissarro rented a house at La Varenne-Saint-Hilaire, opposite Chennevières, 1863-5.

The National Galleries of Scotland

1. Pissarro and Venturi no. 47.
2. Pissarro frequently acknowledged his debt to Courbet, see, for example Pissarro pp. 276, 278 and 322.
3. Lloyd compares no. 12 with Daubigny's *The Banks of the Seine at Bonnières* 1857 (Hellebranth no. 76).
4. Quoted in Grad and Riggs p. 153, where Rousset's photograph *The Islands and the Wood of Chennevières* is reproduced (fig. 85). Rousset also followed Daubigny by studying river scenery from a floating studio.

JEAN-BAPTISTE-CAMILLE COROT

[13] Souvenir des environs du Lac de Nemi

Canvas: 98.5 x 134.5
Signed and dated, lower left: *Corot 1865*
Lit: Robaut no. 1636.

This was exhibited at the Salon in 1865; its title does not translate easily (literally 'Recollection of the surroundings of Lake Nemi'). Around 1850 Corot's style in his

[13]

exhibited works changed profoundly. The titles of many of his later paintings begin with the word *Souvenir*, implying they are landscapes of reflection rather than of observation and in this respect they are similar to the late landscapes of Claude Lorrain. They represent a very personal attempt by Corot to revive the historical landscape. Critics found this painting typical of the repetitiveness of Corot's late work and also complained of its sombre, grey tones. The most favourable comments were those of Thoré, but in 1867, writing again of the *Lac de Nemi* when it was exhibited in the Universal Exhibition, he too, accused Corot of a lack of variation.[1] This work was also included in an exhibition of Corot's paintings at the Ecole des Beaux-Arts in 1875, to which it was lent by the collector Albert Hecht who owned Monet's *Boats in the Pool of London* (no. 90).[2]

The Art Institute of Chicago
(Bequest of Florence S. McCormick)

1. Thoré pp. 223 and 357-8.
2. Other lenders of works by Corot to the 1875 exhibition included Daubigny and the operatic baritone Faure (see nos. 90, 100).

LOUIS-ALEXANDRE DUBOURG

[*14] Sea Bathing at Honfleur

Canvas: 50 x 86
Signed, lower right: *A. Dubourg*
Lit: Bergeret-Gourbin, 1980.

Exhibited at the Salon in 1869, this picture by a close friend and contemporary of Boudin's drew the favourable comment from the critic Alfred Darcel that it was, 'an advertisement for L. A. Dubourg's native town, for it reveals a fact of which we were ignorant, that there was sea bathing at Honfleur, and it reveals it to us with much charm.'[1] The anecdotal nature of the painting and the concentration of large figures on the seashore are more reminiscent of English seaside panoramas[2] than of the atmospheric studies of the Normandy coast by Boudin and Monet. This more formal, finished quality earned Dubourg critical praise at Boudin's expense: 'his

[Dubourg's] paintings recall those of M. E. Boudin, but with more science in the drawing and more seriousness in the execution' (Darcel). Honfleur is one of the prettiest of the coastal towns of Normandy and supported a strong local school of artists in the 19th century, many of whom congregated at the Saint-Siméon farm overlooking Honfleur (no. 55). Dubourg was a prominent member of this school and played a major rôle in establishing a museum in Honfleur devoted to these artists' works. It opened in 1869 and he was its first curator. It is now the Musée Eugène Boudin which held a retrospective exhibition of Dubourg's work in 1985.[3]

Musée Eugène Boudin, Honfleur

1. *L'Echo Honfleurais* 19 June 1869.
2. The most famous examples of which is Frith's *Life at the Seaside, Ramsgate Sands* (Royal Collection).
3. Bergeret-Gourbin, 1985.

CHARLES-FRANCOIS DAUBIGNY

[15] La Frette (View of Herblay)

Panel: 38.8 x 67
Signed and dated, lower right: *Daubigny 1869*
Lit: Hellebranth no. 38.

Although this painting is modest in size, its composition is broad and ambitious. River scenery was frequently depicted in French landscape painting in the 1850s and 60s, particularly by Daubigny, whose example was followed by Pissarro in a number of his early works (no. 12). The view is of the village of Herblay,[1] on the right bank of the Seine, seen across the bend in the river from nearby La Frette. These two villages are to the north-west of Paris, beyond Argenteuil.

The National Galleries of Scotland

1. For other pictures of Herblay, including its distinctive church, see Hellebranth nos. 39-41.

The Sketch

The direct approach to nature which today is so admired in Impressionist landscape was, in many respects, anticipated in the small, preparatory oil-sketches produced by French landscape painters in the late 18th and 19th centuries. Landscape emerged as an important subject in European art in the 17th century and the practice of executing oil studies from nature also originated then. By the late 18th century this custom had become widespread, particularly amongst northern artists working in Italy. Two types of landscape sketch can be distinguished: the study after nature (*étude*), and the compositional sketch (*esquisse*). The *étude* was executed in oils on paper which had been prepared with an oil ground that was tan or beige in colour. It was usually laid-down (*marouflé*) onto canvas or panel. The use of a paper support indicates these sketches were probably considered as coloured drawings rather than small oil-paintings. The sketch encouraged a free, spontaneous approach to nature and it was relatively unfettered by academic dogma. The painter Valenciennes, in his treatise on landscape published in 1800, encouraged the making of rapid sketches which should not be too highly finished, otherwise they would lose the effect (*effet*) in nature they were trying to capture. Much of the history of the landscape sketch is still uncertain. The paper ground was gradually dispensed with and artists began to paint their *études* directly onto canvas or panel. After early experimentation with the *étude* and the *esquisse*, the Impressionists abandoned the sketch and painted directly from nature with little recourse to preparatory studies.

PIERRE-HENRI DE VALENCIENNES

[16] Rome at Sunrise: the Alban Hills in the Distance

Paper on board: 23 x 41.8
Lit: Gowing and Conisbee no. 32.

The view is partly imaginary and is probably taken from the Janiculum; the church of St John Lateran is visible in the distance on the left. It is primarily a study of sky and clouds, a subject on which Valenciennes later advised the reader of his landscape treatise to, 'begin his study with the sky, which gives the tonality for the background'.[1] As recent research has shown,[2] Valenciennes must have made both sketches directly from nature and those which were worked up in the studio, as was probably the case here. Valenciennes first travelled to Italy in 1777, returned to Paris 1780-1 (where he received advice from Vernet), and was back in Italy by Easter 1782. His surviving Italian landscape sketches, the majority of which are now in the Louvre, were executed in 1782-4/5.

Private Collection

1. Valenciennes p. 407.
2. Whitney; Lacambre.

[17] Buildings on the Palatine

Paper on canvas: 23 x 38
Lit: Gowing and Conisbee no. 31.

The identification of the site is uncertain.

Private Collection

FRENCH SCHOOL, LATE 18TH-CENTURY

[18] Vicovaro

Paper on card: 27.5 x 34.5

This sketch was trimmed prior to its purchase by its present owner. On the verso of a damaged section removed from the right-hand side was an ink inscription identifying the site as Vicovaro (in the hills to the east of Rome) and the date as 1787. This was written in a hand that may be identified with that of Louis Gauffier (1762-1801) who arrived in Italy having won the Rome Prize in 1784. He was in Rome until 1793, practising mainly as a history painter, and then moved to Florence to avoid reprisals against French citizens in the wake of the execution of Louis XVI. In Florence he produced portraits of Grand Tourists set against city – and landscapes, and also many fine landscapes of the convent at Vallombrosa. This sketch is a good indication of how strong the tradition of landscape sketching

already was with French artists in the decades prior to the publication in 1800 of Valenciennes's treatise on landscape.

Private Collection

JEAN-JOSEPH-XAVIER BIDAULD

[*19] The Heights of Sannois seen from the Plain of Argenteuil

Paper on canvas: 21.5 x 47.7

Bidauld[1] was the first landscape painter to be elevated to membership of the Académie des Beaux-Arts. This sketch of ca.1798[2] conforms to many of the academic requirements of the landscape sketch. It is fresh, informal and small in scale. It may have been completed in the studio. The area it depicts would be of great importance for Impressionism. Monet lived at Argenteuil, a riverside town to the north-west of Paris, from 1871 to 1878.[3] In 1872 he painted two pictures of the town[4] viewed from Sannois which is on a line of low hills some two miles to the north.

Stoppenbach and Delestre Limited

1. Gutwirth, 1978.
2. Information from François Delestre, based on an unpublished thesis on Bidauld by S. Gutwirth.
3. See Tucker, 1982.
4. Private Collection and Musée d'Orsay, Paris; Wildenstein nos. 219, 220.

JEAN-VICTOR BERTIN

[20] Landscape with Sheep and a Woman Sewing

Canvas: 40.5 x 30.5
Lit: Cormack and Robinson no. 2.

The fine detailed touch of this painting and its studied composition suggest it was probably painted as a small cabinet picture: nevertheless, the intimacy of scale and observation of light demonstrate how such pictures must have benefited from the more spontaneous approach to nature evolved in the landscape sketch. Bertin[1] studied under Valenciennes and in turn taught many artists including Corot,[2] thus forming a link between historical and romantic landscape. His important studio also produced many of the winners of the Rome Prize for landscape. This is probably an early painting.[3]

The Syndics of the Fitzwilliam Museum, Cambridge

1. See Gutwirth, 1974 who includes a partial catalogue of his *oeuvre*.
2. Corot frequented Bertin's studio 1822-5 but deemed it of little worth.
3. Ca. 1800-06, cf. for example, Gutwirth nos. 37, 38, 42, 43.

[20]

[24]

ACHILLE-ETNA MICHALLON

[21] Torrent

Paper on canvas: 38.2 x 30.2
Lit: Gowing and Conisbee no. 78.

The attribution of this sketch was confirmed when it was exhibited in 1978 alongside two sketches[1] by Michallon from the large collection of his work in the Louvre. Michallon was the first winner of the Rome Prize for landscape. Despite his brief career, he was an important linking figure between the first generation of classical landscapists and the more naturalistic approach of Corot. The treatment of water rushing round rocks is similar to that in Corot's early sketch of the *Bridge at Moret* (no. 23).

Private Collection

1. Gowing and Conisbee nos. 76-7.

FRANCOIS-MARIUS GRANET

[22] A Shower of Rain in the Tiber Valley

Paper on canvas: 19 x 37.5
Lit: Pontier no. 79.

After a period of study that included working in David's studio in Paris, Granet travelled to Rome in 1802 with Count Auguste de Forbin and remained there until 1819. He visited Rome again in 1829-30. Although his exhibited work consisted mainly of interiors of churches and monasteries, and of historical scenes, he also painted extensively in the countryside around Rome, producing many beautiful sketches there.

Musée Granet, Aix-en-Provence

JEAN-BAPTISTE-CAMILLE COROT

[23] The Bridge at Moret

Canvas: 25 x 39
Studio stamp lower left.
Lit: Robaut no. 28.

Corot would have learnt the practice of open-air sketching from his first two teachers, Bertin and Michallon, who had both been pupils of Valenciennes. This very early sketch, executed in October 1822 according to Robaut, is understandably rather awkward in manner and lacks the facility Corot would develop during his first visit to Italy 1825-8. The treatment of the water rushing over the weir can be compared to that found in similar sketches by Michallon (no. 21). Moret-sur-Loing is a few miles south-east of Fontainebleau. Its medieval bridge has a mill-house in its centre, the water-wheel of which is visible through the arch on the right in Corot's sketch. The bridge was painted frequently by Sisley in the late 1880s and 90s.

Private Collection

[24] Landscape: Petit-Chaville, near Ville d'Avray

Paper on canvas: 24 x 33
Studio stamp, lower right.
Lit: Robaut no. 16.

This has been compared, in technique, with Corot's famous *Cabassud House*[1] now in the Louvre and both have been dated to 1824-5, just before Corot's first Italian journey. It demonstrates the progress that had been made by Corot in mastering light and tone since the very early and tentative sketch of the *Bridge at Moret* (no. 23). Chaville was a village near Ville d'Avray where Corot lived. It was divided into three parts of which Petit-Chaville was one. According to Robaut, Corot was so attached to this sketch that he bought it back later in his career.

The Visitors of the Ashmolean Museum, Oxford

1. Toussaint, 1975 under no. 3. The Louvre picture is Robaut no. 284.

RICHARD PARKES BONINGTON

[25] Landscape with Mountains

Board: 25.1 x 33
Lit: Spencer no. 270.

Bonington is often regarded more as a French than English painter, his family having moved from Nottingham to France, probably late in 1817. He studied at the Ecole des Beaux-Arts and enrolled in the studio of Baron Gros where fellow students included Isabey and Huet (some of whose later small beach scenes were strongly influenced by Bonington). Much admired by Delacroix, with whom he shared a studio in 1825, Bonington embarked on a visit to Venice in 1826 with their mutual friend Baron Charles Rivet. After a stay of four weeks they travelled back in early June via Genoa, the possible location of this sketch.[1] Although a sketch such as this is very much indebted to the example and writings of Valenciennes,[2] Bonington's rich use of paint is most individual and may have influenced Corot who, in old age, claimed it was the sight of a Bonington watercolour in a Parisian dealer's window that had encouraged him to become a painter.[3]

The National Galleries of Scotland

1. Probably no. 160 (*Environs of Genoa*) in the Bonington sale, Sotheby's, 29 June 1829, bought Lawrence. The sketch was bought in 1910 by the National Gallery of Scotland from Alexander Reid, the Scottish dealer who did so much to introduce the work of the Impressionists to British collections.

12. Camille Pissarro, *The Banks of the Marne at Chennevières*

19. Jean-Joseph-Xavier Bidauld, *The Heights of Sannois seen from the Plain of Argenteuil*

35. Eugène Delacroix, *The Sea from the Heights at Dieppe*

[26]

2. Suggested by Pointon p. 110 who also, less plausibly, compares no. 25 with the oil-sketches of Bertin and d'Aligny. She is surely correct, however, in suggesting it was executed on the spot and not in the studio.
3. Dubuisson and Hughes p. 51.

JEAN-BAPTISTE-CAMILLE COROT

[26] Lago di Piediluco, Umbria

Canvas: 22 x 41
Studio stamp, lower left.
Lit: Robaut no. 123.[1]

Corot's first and most important visit to Italy lasted from late 1825 to mid-1828. He made two sketching trips north of Rome in the summer of 1826, the second of which was in the Terni region from July to mid-October. He stayed in the picturesque village of Papigno which was much frequented by landscape artists. Piediluco, the subject of this luminous sketch, is in the mountains above Papigno.

The Visitors of the Ashmolean Museum, Oxford

1. According to whom several copies were painted after no. 26.
2. A. and R. Jullien, 1982, who identify the site from which no. 26 was painted as that now occupied by a water-sports club.

THEODORE CARUELLE D'ALIGNY

[27] Avenue in the Forest of Fontainebleau

Paper on board: 60 x 46.5
Lit: Gerkens and Heiderich pp. 16-17.

Probably executed around 1830, this is an unusually large outdoor oil-sketch. Its freshness of observation, particularly the light falling on the roadway, anticipates Monet's paintings of 1865 in the Forest. In many respects d'Aligny's career was similar to that of Corot. Both travelled to Italy (they met there in 1825) and widely in France, and both worked extensively in and around Fontainebleau. Their sketches from nature are quite similar, but in their exhibited work they differed. D'Aligny often produced prettified classical landscapes that recall Nicolas Poussin, whereas Corot's arcadian visions are reminiscent of Claude Lorrain.

Kunsthalle, Bremen

FRANCOIS-MARIUS GRANET

[28] Landscape

Paper on card: 19.5 x 29.7
Lit: Pontier no. 78.

This beautifully study of the edge of a wood is comparable, especially in the watery lighting effects, to the many watercolours Granet executed of the parks and woods around Versailles 1833-47, where King Louis-Philippe entrusted him with the organisation of the Museum of French History. Granet finally retired to Aix in 1847.[1]

Musée Granet, Aix-en-Provence

1. For the most recent biography of the artist see Coutagne pp. 122-30.

[29]

[30]

JEAN-BAPTISTE-CAMILLE COROT

[29] The Chestnut Grove

Canvas: 34 x 48.9
Signed, lower left: *COROT*
Lit: Robaut no. 296; Cormack and Robinson no. 13.

According to Robaut, this was painted shortly after Corot's return to France from his second trip to Italy in 1834. The landscape is of the Morvan or the Auvergne, both of which Corot visited at that time. Corot's later sketches acquired the grey tones that became so characteristic of all his work. In this sketch the observation of colour and light, which comes from behind the trees, is still remarkably fresh. By contrast, a sketch of the Morvan, *Peasants under the Trees at Dawn*,[1] dated to the early 1840s and showing similar lighting, is much greyer and more limited in colour.

The Syndics of the Fitzwilliam Museum, Cambridge

1. National Gallery, London; Robaut no. 431.

PIERRE-ETIENNE-THEODORE
ROUSSEAU

[30] Panoramic Landscape

Paper on canvas: 25.7 x 54.9
Inscribed, along lower edge, with place names: *Ticharminil*(?), *flavigny* and *Morneville*.
Lit: Green no. 20.

This probably dates from 1834 when Rousseau made a journey from Paris to the Jura. Flavigny-sur-Ozerain is a village in Burgundy, between Tonnerre and Dijon. The use of a long horizontal format for a landscape sketch was ultimately Netherlandish in origin. Its merit lay in the amount of topographical information it could contain.

The Syndics of the Fitzwilliam Museum, Cambridge

[31] Landscape

Paper on panel: 24 x 35

This may have been executed in the Forest of Fontainebleau but its location is uncertain.

Private Collection

FRANCOIS-MARIUS GRANET

[32] Landscape in the Countryside at Aix, Malvalat

Canvas: 27.2 x 35.1
Lit: Pontier no. 54.

The structure of the landscape in this sketch shows how the rocky, mountainous terrain round Aix could approximate to that of Italy. The composition is similar to the Italian sketches of Bonington and Corot. The buildings in the mid-distance of this sketch include the chapel of St. Jean de la Pinette where Granet and his wife are buried. It is difficult to date Granet's sketches of his native Aix for he is known to have visited it on numerous occasions after his return from his first major period in Italy, 1802-19.

Musée Granet, Aix-en-Provence

[33] Mte. Sainte-Victoire seen from a Courtyard at Malvalat

Canvas: 32.5 x 41
Lit: Pontier no. 69.

Granet acquired a country house at Malvalat near Aix in 1831. This is one of numerous sketches he made of the Mte. Sainte-Victoire to the east of Aix. It was a subject that was painted many times by southern painters[1] before Cézanne began his long and famous series of pictures of it later in the century. Apart from 199 drawings he bequeathed to the Louvre, Granet left the rest of the contents of his studio to his native town of Aix. In his youth Cézanne studied at the drawing academy in Aix under Professor Gibert, who was also curator of the Aix Museum (re-named the Musée Granet in 1949). Cézanne is known to have admired the Granet sketches which were on display there.[2]

Musée Granet, Aix-en-Provence

1. For example, Prosper Grésy's (1804-1874) *The Mte. Sainte-Victoire and the hamlet of Bonfillons* in the Musée Granet.
2. Coutagne p. 133.

EUGENE BOUDIN

[34] The Tower of François Ier, Le Havre

Panel: 16 x 38.5
Signed, lower right: *E. Boudin;* and dated, lower left: *1852*
Lit: Schmit no. 8.

This is one of a pair[1] of oil-sketches by Boudin of the François Ier tower. The tower was begun in 1517; when this sketch was painted it was used as a semaphore post at the entrance to the port of Le Havre. It was already

[33]

[34]

a popular subject with both French and English artists. It was demolished between 1861 and 1867.[2] This sketch displays a technique which captures perfectly the fresh sea air of Le Havre with flags flying in the breeze, ships in the estuary with their sails fully filled and a rapidly changing sky. The two sketches of 1852 show that, relatively early in his career, Boudin had mastered the open-air oil-sketch. His light, airy pictures influenced the young Monet, who grew up in Le Havre and received advice and encouragement from the older painter.[3]

Musée des Beaux-Arts 'André Malraux', Le Havre

1. The other is also in the Musée des Beaux-Arts, Le Havre. Schmit no. 7. They are the earliest surviving dated works by Boudin.
2. Information from M. Franc Duboc, Sous-Archiviste, Musées du Havre.
3. Monet *Interview*, 1900, reprinted in Nochlin pp. 37-8.

44

EUGENE DELACROIX

[*35] The Sea from the Heights at Dieppe

Panel: 35 x 51
Verso, studio stamp
Lit: Robaut and Chesneau, no. 1245; Sérullaz.

Delacroix first visited the Normandy coast in 1813 and returned on numerous occasions. These visits are listed by Sérullaz who dates this sketch to either 1852 or 1854. Delacroix was at Dieppe in both years and made the following observations in his *Journal* 14 September 1852; 'It was from this side of the sea that I made a study from memory: golden sky, boats waiting for the tide so as to get back to port'.[1] And in August 1854, writing in Paris before a trip to Dieppe: 'The same is true of the waves of the sea, which divide themselves into little waves, again subdividing, and individually presenting the same accidents of light and the same pattern.'[2] It is difficult to assess whether a sketch such as this, or Delacroix's many similar marine watercolours, influenced the young Impressionists. Delacroix compiled many notes on colour in the 1850s and some were published in 1865. They reveal a concern with issues that also preoccupied the Impressionists: the banishing of dark, earth colours; the necessity of relying on the three primary colours; the laws of complementary contrast.[3] Colour theory was widely discussed in the 19th century in artistic and scientific circles. The young Impressionists could have seen this sketch in the posthumous Delacroix exhibition held in Paris in 1864[4] and a seascape by Monet of 1866 shows a concern with comparable effects.[5] The closest parallel to Delacroix's painting, however, is found in one by Chintreuil (no. 42). Delacroix was one of many artists who sketched the Normandy coast in the 1850s. Boudin was already making out-of-doors sketches there and Sérullaz quotes from an entry dated 12 December 1854 in one of Boudin's notebooks, 'The sea was superb – at first silvery, the sky was *soft* – it then turned to yellow; it became warm, delicate, then the sun, in going down, cast beautiful purple shades over everything'.[6]

Musée du Louvre, Paris

1. Delacroix I p. 488.
2. Delacroix II pp. 227-28.
3. See Johnson p. 104.
4. *Oeuvres d'Eugène Delacroix*, Paris, Société Nationale des Beaux-Arts, 26, bd. des Italiens, 1864, no. 149 (*Souvenir de Dieppe*).
5. Ordrupgardsamling, Copenhagen; Wildenstein no. 72. A pointed comparison with Monet was made in the 1970 exhibition *Delacroix et l'Impressionisme* Musée Delacroix, Paris in which the Dieppe sketch was hung directly above Monet's famous *Impression: Sunrise* (Wildenstein no. 263).
6. Passage on folio 29 recto of a notebook of 65 pages, now in the Louvre, quoted by Sérullaz p. 12.

PIERRE-ETIENNE-THEODORE ROUSSEAU

[36] Landscape with Red Sunset

Panel: 30.5 x 45.8
Signed, lower left: *TH.R.*
Lit: Gillow p. 914.

Dated by Herbert to the early 1850s,[1] this relatively large sketch exhibits, in its extraordinary use of red, an extremely emotional use of colour. Critics and theorists in the 19th century often wrote of the need for feeling or *sentiment* in a landscape. The liberation of colour from a purely descriptive function would be investigated in much greater detail in the later 19th and early 20th centuries.

York City Art Gallery

1. Letter in York Art Gallery files.

[37] The Plain of Chailly

Panel: 29 x 37 (painted area 27.2 x 35.2)
Signed, lower left: *TH. Rousseau*
Lit: Scrase no. 19.

This sketch has traditionally been identified as of Chailly and dated 1833,[1] when Rousseau first visited this small village near Barbizon in the Forest of Fontainebleau. Recently, however, Miquel has suggested it was painted in 1844 and shows the scenery of the Landes in south-west France;[2] whereas Green has retained the location as Chailly but dated it to the 1850s.[3] Green also describes it as an '*ébauche*-type work', thereby equating it with the academic practice of laying in, with thinned paint, the basic areas of tone in a picture before adding the darks and the highlights. A number of these *ébauches* by Rousseau survive and it is interesting to compare the simple accenting of tufts of grass and other features of the landscape with similar effects in two of Monet's Argenteuil landscapes.[4]

The Syndics of the Fitzwilliam Museum, Cambridge

1. Followed by Herbert, 1962 no. 87.
2. Miquel, 1975, III, p. 445 as *Le marais dans les Landes*.
3. Green no. 36.
4. Private Collection and Musée d'Orsay, Paris; Wildenstein nos. 219-20.

ADOLPHE-FELIX CALS

[38] The Plain of Colombes

Paper on panel: 10.8 x 40
Signed and dated, lower left: *Cals 5 Août '56*
Lit: Baer no. 7.

[37]

[40]

The Plain of Colombes is on the opposite side of the Seine to Argenteuil, north-west of Paris, an area that Monet painted extensively in the 1870s. Cals had executed open-air landscapes as early as 1830, and in 1848 he met the dealer Père Martin at his shop in the rue Mogador. Martin not only bought from Corot, Millet and Rousseau but would later support Cézanne, Monet and Pissarro. One of his most important clients was Count Armand Doria who invited Cals to his château at Orrouy where the artist stayed 1859-70. Based at Orrouy, Cals made frequent trips to the Normandy coast where he met Boudin, Courbet and the young Monet. He eventually moved to Honfleur entering the Saint-Siméon farm circle there.

Mr and Mrs Jack Baer

CAMILLE PISSARRO

[39] The Port-Marly Road

Panel: 22.8 x 35.1
Initialled, lower right: *C.P.*
Lit: Lloyd, 1984 no. 10.

Like the sketch for the *Towpath* (no. 10), this is one of Pissarro's few surviving compositional sketches (*esquisses*) for a larger picture, in this instance one that was either lost or never completed. It dates from the mid- to late 1860s. Port-Marly is on the left bank of the Seine near Louveciennes, to which Pissarro moved in 1869. The device of showing the road at an oblique angle would be repeated by Pissarro in many pictures of the late 1860s and early 70s.

The Syndics of the Fitzwilliam Museum, Cambridge

EUGENE CASTELNAU

[40] Sketch near Montpellier

Canvas: 23 x 42 cm
Signed, lower right: *E. Castelnau*
Lit: Marandel no. 61.

Although an exhibition[1] in 1977 at the Musée Fabre drew attention to Castelnau's achievement, his work remains little studied. He belonged to a strong tradition of landscape painting in southern France which included such artists as Granet, Guigou, Cézanne and Bazille. Bazille, though younger, was a close friend of Castelnau's and, like him, a native of Montpellier. Castelnau spent most of his life in Languedoc, apart from a brief period of study in Paris and a trip to Italy 1853-4. The influence of Bazille's lighter palette is evident in Castelnau's treatment of the hot, arid southern landscape. Earlier works by Castelnau are descriptive and detailed with little sense of atmosphere.

Musée Fabre, Montpellier

1. Dejean.

FREDERIC BAZILLE

[41] Studies for a 'Gathering of the Grapes'

Canvas: 38 x 92
Lit: Daulte, 1952 pp. 181-2; Marandel no. 34.

Although framed together, these are two separate studies (*études*) for the landscape in a painting of *The Gathering of the Grapes*[1] which was probably intended for the Salon. Bazille may have begun it in 1868 but it was never completed. Three pencil sketches in one of his two surviving Louvre sketchbooks reveal the ambitious, formal nature of this composition.[2] The choice of subject may have been influenced by similar pictures that Jules Breton and Daubigny, amongst others, had already exhibited with success at the Salon. The careful

[41]

[42]

preparations for this and other works after 1865 show Bazille reverting to traditional academic practice by using small open-air sketches in preparation for an elaborate final picture. Unlike the other Impressionist landscape painters, Bazille's fascination with the scenery of the north and the Ile de France was brief and he returned to his native south. Both these views were taken from the hillside at the Bionne estate which belonged to M. Tissié, the father-in-law of Bazille's brother, Marc. In the foreground are the autumn vines and in the distance the plain of Launac, near Montpellier, and the mountain of La Gardiole.

Musée Fabre, Montpellier

1. According to a note in one of Bazille's Louvre sketchbooks (RF 5259 f. 67 verso) he was contemplating both large and small versions.
2. Louvre sketchbook RF 5260 nos. 7, 14, 19. The other Louvre sketchbook is RF 5259, the illustrations to both are listed and reproduced in Marandel, pp. 214-27.

ANTOINE CHINTREUIL

[42] Sunset at Sea

Canvas: 24 x 36
Signed, lower right: *Chintreuil* with studio stamp on the stretcher.
Lit: Possibly De La Fizelière no. 457 (*Pleine mer, effet du soir; Boulogne* 25 x 37)

This was possibly executed in either 1869 or 1872[1] when Chintreuil is known to have stayed in Boulogne. It bears obvious comparison with Delacroix's earlier Dieppe sketch (no. 35), but it is softer and gentler in handling, the brushstrokes are more blended and less visible, the colours lighter and daintier.

Kunsthalle, Bremen

1. See Miquel's biography of the artist in Baudson pp. 89-111.

Barbizon and mid-century Landscape

By the middle of the 19th century landscape painting in France had diversified considerably from the academic, historical landscape which had dominated the genre at the beginning of the century. At the great 1855 Universal Exhibition in Paris many critics perceived landscape as occupying a place equal, if not superior to, historical and religious painting. Its growing popularity was even considered to be politically subversive by reactionary elements in French artistic circles. Landscape was seen to challenge the academic hierarchy of art and its lack of esoteric subject-matter encouraged the suspicion that it might be adopted as a people's art. The critic Castagnary, a friend of Courbet and Millet, claimed that landscape painters were of the people because, 'they have shared with us humiliations and miseries. The public acclaim them, but the Institute [of France] rebuffs them and the administration turns them away'. The major figures in the emancipation of landscape were the painters who belonged to the community of artists which came to be known as the School of Barbizon and who lived and worked in the village of that name in the Forest of Fontainebleau south-east of Paris. The landscapes which Rousseau, Diaz, Dupré, Troyon and others produced there from around 1840 were inspired by the forest scenes of the 17th-century Dutch masters. The Barbizon circle also included Corot, Daubigny and Millet. They lived modestly and congregated at the Auberge Ganne for food, drink and conversation. The Forest itself was already a well-known tourist attraction that had spawned guide-books and paths specially marked-out for visitors. Although they affected a rural life-style, the artists of Barbizon were essentially part of an urban reaction against the rapid industrialisation and expansion of Paris. Their forest scenes were bought by the Parisians whose city the painters had forsaken. On a broader front, a nationalistic pride in the landscape of France developed under successive political regimes in the 19th century. Regional schools of landscape painting were formed in centres such as Honfleur, Grenoble, Lyons and Marseilles. Artists travelled extensively. Rousseau painted in the Landes in the south-west and Corot worked in many areas of France. The Impressionists absorbed certain features of style from their immediate predecessors, Corot and Daubigny particularly, but their patterns of movement and travel were different. Only Pissarro, during his second period at Pontoise, favoured the idea, embodied in Barbizon, of a rural community of artists. None of the Impressionists were great travellers in their early years: they concentrated instead on Paris and its suburbs and on the tourist towns and villages of the Normandy coast.

GEORGES MICHEL

[43] Storm near Montmartre

Canvas: 68.6 x 138.5

Michel's art anticipated the interest of the Barbizon School in Dutch 17th-century landscape. He was employed for a time as restorer of the Netherlandish paintings in the Louvre.[1] This splendid example is particularly indebted to Rembrandt and the storm effects recall the Dutch master's celebrated etching, *The Three Trees*. Michel endlessly explored the region round Montmartre (he was known as the 'Ruisdael of Montmartre') which in the early 19th century remained wild and undeveloped, outside the confines of the city of Paris to which it seemed the nearest rural village – in some ways a precursor of Barbizon. By the 1860s and 70s Montmartre had been transformed. Its population had greatly increased and it had become a popular area for artists and writers.

Leeds City Art Galleries

1. See J. Foucart, 'De Hollandse inspiratie' in Sillevis and Kraan pp. 21-34.

JEAN-BAPTISTE-CAMILLE COROT

[*44] Ville d'Avray, Entrance to a Wood

Canvas: 46 x 34.9
Signed, in a later hand, lower right: *COROT*
Lit: Robaut no. 33; Thompson and Brigstocke p. 18.

In 1817 Corot's father purchased a house in the country at Ville d'Avray, to the west of Paris. The scenery there was gentler and more cultivated than that of the Forest of Fontainebleau which would later fascinate the Barbizon School. Dated by Robaut 1823-5, this is an important early work, executed before Corot's first trip to Italy in 1825. Although somewhat hesitant in touch, it already exhibits many of the most attractive characteristics of Corot's work, such as a brightness of tone and a concern with the effects of light falling across a landscape. The vertical composition, with a tall tree as the dominating motif, is reminiscent of English painting, Constable in particular,[1] though Corot's view of nature was always softer and more gentle than that of the English artist. The 1824 Salon was referred to by a number of writers as the 'English Salon'[2] on account of the number of English works exhibited there, including Constable's celebrated *Hay Wain*. Corot would already have been familiar with English painting, however, for the 1824 Salon was really a culmination of French enthusiasm for the English manner. Robaut states that when the picture was owned by the writer Alfred Sensier it was altered by Diaz. Infra-red examination confirms Robaut's account. The original composition is recorded in a copy now in the Gothenburg Art Gallery, Sweden (fig. 5).[3] The woman and the cow on the right were replaced with a seated woman, the small cottage and

standing figure on the left painted over with more foliage and a figure was also added in the far distance.

The National Galleries of Scotland

1. Beckett; R. Hoozee, 'Constable en de Engelse landschapskunst' in Sillevis and Kraan pp. 35-45.
2. See Pointon pp. 80-82.
3. *Forest Path, Ville d'Avray* canvas, 48 x 37. The Edinburgh painting was cleaned 1986, Diaz's alterations have not been removed.

Fig. 5. Corot, Studio of, *Forest Path, Ville d'Avray*, Gothenburg Art Gallery, Sweden.

[45] The Quarry of La Chaise-à-Marie at Fontainebleau

Canvas: 34 x 59
Signed, lower right: *COROT*; and inscribed and dated, lower left: *Fontainebleau/juin 1831*.
Lit: Robaut no. 271; Sillevis and Kraan no. 13.

Corot began to work regularly in the Forest of Fontainebleau in 1830 and continued to do so for the rest of his career. Both Corot and d'Aligny frequently depicted the quarries there, though the latter's pictures of Fontainebleau,[1] with their brighter lighting, smoother finish and more classical composition, are more reminiscent of Italy (where the two artists had met in the 1820s) than were Corot's. The stone at Fontainebleau was quarried for use on the roads and for the construction industries in Paris.

Museum voor Schone Kunsten, Ghent

1. For example d'Aligny's *View of the quarries of Mont Saint-Père in the Forest of Fontainebleau*, Musée Bargoin, Clermont-Ferrand, Aubrun no. 2.

[46]

[47]

EUGENE DELACROIX

[46] Pyrenean Landscape

Canvas: 39.5 x 54.3
Lit: Busch no. 382.

Delacroix spent about a month taking the waters at Eaux-Bonnes in the Pyrenees in the summer of 1845. He had suffered from throat trouble since 1835. Although disenchanted with his fellow patients, he found the mountain scenery there magnificent. This painting was probably executed after his return to Paris, for he had not taken painting materials with him to the Pyrenees. Mountains were rarely depicted in 19th-century French paintings, though they were often shown in prints.[1] The sublime in nature did not capture the French imagination to the same degree as it did the German and the English; nor did it appeal to the Impressionists who would be much more concerned with the urban and the suburban, with the near and the mundane rather than the distant and infinite.

Dr Peter Nathan, Zürich

1. Grad and Riggs pp. 35-51.

HENRI-JOSEPH HARPIGNIES

[47] Crémieu

Canvas: 38 x 46

Signed and dated, lower left: *Hiharpignies 1847;* inscribed, lower right: *Cremieux*[sic]; inscribed on the stretcher, in pencil: *Mon/.../Etude à/Cremieu/en/1847/ ma/.../ & Maître/=/Harpignies/...*
Lit: Scrase no. 14.

See no. 48.

The Syndics of the Fitzwilliam Museum, Cambridge

[48] Cliffs near Crémieu

Canvas: 32 x 46
Signed and dated, lower left: *h'harpignies. 1847;* inscribed on the stretcher, in pencil: *Seconde étude faite à ... en 1847,* and *mai 1893*

These are two early works by Harpignies which, to judge from the pencil inscriptions on the stretchers, remained with him for most, if not all, of his life. Harpignies entered the Parisian studio of the established landscape painter Jean-Alexis Achard in 1846. In July 1847 they travelled to Lyons and then spent August to October sketching in nearby Optevoz and Crémieu in the company of the Lyons painter Paul Flandrin. Similar accounts of the execution of these two sketches can be found in Harpignies's unpublished *Journal*[1] and in an article by Armand Silvestre[2] on Harpignies of 1883. A drawing of 1841 (fig. 6)[3] by Eugène Bléry (1805-1887) of Crémieu shows, from further away, the same gorge and buildings as are depicted in no. 48. The region around Crémieu, to the east of Lyons, was popular with landscape artists and its hilly and rocky landscape was often compared to that of Italy. Daubigny described it in 1849 as, 'a magnificent region. It has an amazing savagery, reminiscent of Gaspard, Poussin and Salvator'.[4] The style of Harpignies' two paintings is a fascinating mid-century mixture. The brilliant lighting and smoothly intricate areas, such as the trees to the right of no. 48, are reminiscent of the classical landscapist Flandrin. The emphasis placed on the rocky scenery, however, is similar to that found in the mountainous landscapes Courbet painted near his native town of Ornans in the Jura.

The National Galleries of Scotland

1. Quoted in Miquel, 1975 p. 775.
2. Silvestre, I am indebted to Richard Thomson for this reference.
3. Pencil: 27.2 x 42.7, inscribed and signed, lower left: *Vue de la ville de Cremieu prise du Moutures/12 Juin 1841/E. Blery,* Huntington Library, California. I am grateful to Nadia E. Awad for details of this.
4. Letter to Geoffrey-Dechaume 9 November, Moreau-Nélaton, 1925 pp. 53-4.

PHILIPPE ROUSSEAU

[49] A Valley

Canvas: 81 x 99.5
Signed, lower left: *Ph. Rousseau*
Lit: Davies p. 125; Weisberg 1981/2 no. 155.

Rousseau became well-known as a still-life painter, but his early submissions to the Salon between 1834 and 1841 were all landscapes. The free brushwork and brilliant lighting of this picture anticipate Impressionism. This type of composition, with its high horizon and plunging middle ground, is relatively unusual but can be found later in certain landscapes by Millet, Pissarro and Cézanne.

The National Gallery, London

JEAN-BAPTISTE-CAMILLE COROT

[*50] Ville d'Avray, the Cabassud House

Canvas: 65 x 90
Signed, lower left: *COROT*
Lit: Robaut no. 516.

This is one of a number of pictures[1] by Corot that show the view from the Corot family property at Ville d'Avray towards the Cabassud House (named after its owner). The connecting causeway was built in 1849 on the orders of the local authorities as part of the improvements made to the ponds at Ville d'Avray. This painting

[48]

Fig. 6. Eugène Bléry, *View of Crémieu* 1841,
Huntington Library, California.

[49]

[51]

probably dates from 1850-5.[2] As has been often observed, Corot's frequent depiction of Ville d'Avray throughout his career can be compared to Cézanne's lifelong fascination with his family's property at the Jas de Bouffan near Aix. Corot and his sister inherited the Ville d'Avray house on their father's death in 1847.

The Searle Collection

1. The best-known is that in the Musée du Louvre, Paris, Robaut no. 284, dated by Toussaint, 1975 no. 3 to 1824-5.
2. Toussaint, 1975 under no. 36.

'ADOLPHE' HERVIER

[51] Village Scene: Barbizon

Panel: 12.7 x 30.5
Signed, lower right: *HERVIER*
Lit: Weisberg, 1981/2 no. 157.

The viewpoint in this little sketch is artificially raised and the street opens out to be much wider than it really was. Both these devices show Hervier's indebtedness to Dutch landscapes which influenced all the Barbizon painters. The street is virtually empty, giving the

impression of a quiet, rural retreat. In fact, by the 1850s (to which this panel is usually dated), Barbizon was a flourishing and busy resort for tourists and artists and Millet and Rousseau had already settled there. The railway from Paris had been extended to nearby Fontainebleau in 1849 and foreign, as well as French, painters were visiting the Forest in increasing numbers. The Emperor declared the Forest an 'artistic reservation' in 1853.

Glasgow Museum and Art Gallery

GUSTAVE COURBET

[52] The Shore at Palavas

Canvas: 27 x 46
Signed, lower right: *G. Courbet*; and dated, lower left: . .54
Lit: Fernier no. 150; Bowness and Toussaint, 1977/8 no. 36.

Courbet's friendship with the collector Alfred Bruyas, who acquired this painting, began in 1853 and the following year Bruyas invited the painter to his home in

[52]

55

Montpellier where he stayed from May to September 1854. Courbet celebrated his arrival there with his well-known masterpiece *The Meeting* or *Bonjour Monsieur Courbet*.[1] After meeting Bruyas he confronted the sea, according to the evidence of this painting.[2] In a letter to Jules Vallès he wrote, 'The sea's voice is tremendous, but not loud enough to drown the voice of Fame, crying my name to the entire world'. Courbet is dwarfed, but not humbled by the immensity of Nature, to whom he holds his hat in joyous salute.

Musée Fabre, Montpellier

1. Musée Fabre, Montpellier; Fernier no. 149.
2. For other marines he painted at this time see Fernier nos. 151-4. He had already painted the Normandy coast in the 1840s and was later portrayed there by Whistler in his *Harmony in Blue and Silver: Trouville 1865* (Isabella Stewart Gardner Museum, Boston; McLaren Young no. 64) in a composition which seems to pay homage to no. 52.

CHARLES-FRANCOIS DAUBIGNY

[53] Gobelle's Mill at Optevoz

Canvas: 57.8 x 92.7
Signed, lower left: *C. Daubigny*
Lit: Sterling and Salinger pp. 95-6; Hellebranth no. 518.

This is one of two major versions of this subject, the other, which is signed and dated 1857, is in the Philadelphia Museum of Art.[1] According to Herbert,[2] the Philadelphia version (and presumably the same is true here) was a studio picture based on sketches made at Optevoz in 1852. Herbert also sees the influence of Courbet's brushwork in these pictures. On Optevoz see no. 54.

Metropolitan Museum of Art, New York
(*Bequest of Robert Graham Dun, 1911*)

1. Hellebranth no. 524.
2. Herbert, 1962 no. 22.

[54] The Weir at Optevoz

Canvas: 49 x 73
Signed and dated, lower left: *Daubigny, 1859*
Lit: Hellebranth no. 525.

The landscape round the village of Optevoz, to the east of Lyons and just a few miles north-west of Crémieu, was popular with artists of the generation prior to the Impressionists, both those of the nearby Lyons School and those who visited the area. Daubigny had first worked in the Optevoz/Crémieu district in 1849 and was there again in 1852 when he met Corot. On the latter visit he wrote, 'I leave tomorrow for Optevoz, care of M. Giroux, inn-keeper, where I have begun the studies. It is a very beautiful region, much superior to Crémieu. There are marshes and magnificent backgrounds'.[1] His next visit was in 1854, 'the country-side round Optevoz has never been so beautiful and I am sure I am going to do good things there'.[2] Daubigny painted the weir on a number of occasions, his most important version was commissioned by the State in June 1854 and admired by Gautier when it was exhibited at the Universal Exhibition in 1855. It was bought by the Luxembourg Museum and is now in Rouen.[3] This is a smaller version of the subject. Daubigny was again in Optevoz in 1859 with the Lyons landscape painter Adolphe Appian who submitted a painting of the weir to the Salon that year. Daubigny's painting is not just a repetition of his 1855 picture but a reworking of the subject. Courbet also painted a similar view of the weir.[4]

Musée du Louvre, Paris

1. 20 July to Geoffroy-Dechaume, Moreau-Nélaton, 1925, p. 57.
2. 30 September to Geoffroy-Dechaume, Fidell-Beaufort and Bailly-Herzberg, p. 259.
3. Musée des Beaux-Arts, Rouen; Hellebranth no. 520; see also nos. 527-9 for other versions.
4. Neue Pinakothek, Munich; Fernier no. 158.

EUGENE ISABEY

[55] The Saint-Siméon Farm

Canvas: 30 x 41
Monogram lower left; studio stamp lower right.
Lit: Miquel, 1980 X no. 429.

Between ca. 1855 and 1875 the Saint-Siméon farm,[1] run by 'Mère Toutain', was a celebrated meeting-place on the Normandy coast for artists, writers, musicians and collectors and was an important centre for the exchange of ideas. It was the equivalent of the 'Auberge Ganne' at Barbizon and the artists who frequented it were dubbed the 'Barbizon School of the North' or the 'Saint-Siméon School'. The farm is about a mile west of Honfleur on the Côte de Grace and overlooks the Seine estuary. The Normandy coast had first been explored by English artists in the early 19th century. Isabey provides an interesting link between generations for he had been taught by Bonington and, in turn, was the master of Jongkind, one of the most important of the pre-Impressionists. Saint-Siméon was frequented by a wide variety of landscape painters including Boudin, Cals, Courbet, Daubigny, Diaz, Dubourg and Isabey and, amongst the Impressionists, Monet, Bazille and, much later in 1903, Pissarro who lamented that the new proprietors had 'put the place in good order'[2] (today it is a fine but expensive hotel). In its heyday in 1865 it was described as, 'An honest-to-goodness farm, I assure you, and in the most charming site in the world';[3] whilst Boudin, rather proprietorially, recalled, 'One could make a beautiful legend out of the inn at Saint-Siméon. So many famous people went there after I had discovered it.'[4]

Private Collection

1. Fully discussed in Cunningham.
2. Pissarro p. 357.
3. Delvau.
4. Jean-Aubry p. 33.

44. Jean-Baptiste-Camille Corot, *Ville d'Avray, Entrance to a Wood*

50. Jean-Baptiste-Camille Corot, *Ville d'Avray, the Cabassud House*

61. Frédéric Bazille, *Landscape at Chailly*

62. Virgile Narcisse Diaz de la Peña, *Stormy Landscape*

[54]

CONSTANT TROYON

[56] Return from Work

Canvas: 64.8 x 81.3
Signed, lower left: *C. TROYON*
Lit: Thompson, J. no. 69; Sillevis and Kraan no. 97.

Troyon was primarily a painter of rural and animal scenes but his paintings exhibit a concern with light that must have attracted the Impressionists. Monet and Boudin both expressed admiration for his work and received advice from him. He was closely associated with the Barbizon School and his work was widely imitated.

The National Galleries of Scotland

ANTOINE CHINTREUIL

[57] The Ruins of Montchauvet

Canvas: 40 x 64
Signed, lower right: *Chintreuil*
Lit: De La Fizelière no. 279.

This was recorded in De La Fizelière as belonging to Daubigny by 1874. The two artists had first met in 1850. Chintreuil's woodland scenes were much lighter in tone and colour than those of the Barbizon School. The ruins of Montchauvet[1] are all but obscured by trees in this painting. In his 1859 Salon Baudelaire had regretted the passing of the 'landscape of Romanticism, ... But surely our landscape painters are far too herbiverous in their diet? They never willingly take their nourishment from ruins...'[2].

Gallery Bruno Meissner, Zürich

1. For Montchauvet see also De La Fizelière nos. 309, 331, 338, 378, and Baudson no. 134.
2. Baudelaire p. 201.

VIRGILE NARCISSE DIAZ DE LA PEÑA

[58] Figure in a Woodland Clearing

Canvas: 40.5 x 49.5
Signed and dated, lower right: *N Diaz '64*.

This is a typical small painting by Diaz of the kind which was popular with collectors. In the latter part of his career his work sold well.

Private Collection

CAMILLE PISSARRO

[59] Woodland Scene ('Sous-bois')

Panel: 26.5 x 21
Signed, lower left: *C. Pissarro*
Lit: Pissarro and Venturi no. 38; Lloyd, 1984 no. 5.

This is an early exercise by Pissarro dated by Lloyd to ca. 1864. Although the subject and composition are derived from Corot and Daubigny, the greens and the distinct, flicked brushwork are more reminiscent of the latter. There are smoothly brushed-in passages, however, which, together with some of the lighter yellow-greens and soft blues suggest Pissarro had also looked at Manet's *Déjeuner sur l'Herbe* which had been exhibited at the Salon des Refusés in 1863.

Mr and Mrs Tim Rice

ALFRED SISLEY

[60] Avenue of Trees near a Small Town

Canvas: 45 x 59.5
Signed, lower right: *Sisley*
Lit: Gerkens and Heiderich p. 307; Lloyd, 1985 no. 1.

The date most recently proposed for this painting is ca. 1865 or earlier.[1] Like all the Impressionists at the beginning of their careers, Sisley explored a number of artists' styles before arriving at his own. This painting displays a variety of influences. The brushwork and colouring of the lower part of the picture are particularly indebted to Daubigny, whilst the dappled handling of the foliage comes from Corot.[2]

Kunsthalle, Bremen

1. Lloyd, 1985.
2. Sisley's absorption of Corot's decorative late style could have been stimulated by his friend Renoir whose very early *The Clearing* (Vollard no. 545) of ca. 1860 already exhibits Corot-like foliage.

FREDERIC BAZILLE

[*61] Landscape at Chailly

Canvas: 82 x 105
Signed and dated, lower left: *F. Bazille, 1865*
Lit: Daulte, 1952 p. 171; Marandel no. 14; Brettell and Shaefer no. 7.

The Impressionists' most prolonged contact with the scenery made famous by the artists of the Barbizon School took place in 1865. The young painters spent the summer in the Forest of Fontainebleau. Sisley and Renoir were based in Marlotte, whilst Monet and Bazille were in Chailly-en-Bière. Monet was preoccupied with making studies for his large painting of an open-air picture in the Forest, the *Déjeuner sur l'Herbe* (for

which Bazille posed) which was intended for the 1866 Salon. Bazille and Monet had already worked in the Forest in 1863 when Bazille wrote to his mother: 'Certain parts of the forest are truly wonderful. We can't even imagine such oak trees in Montpellier. In spite of their great fame, the rocks are not so beautiful. One could easily find more imposing ones around our city.'[1] References in letters from his 1865 visit indicate he made a number of studies (*études*) there. *Landscape at Chailly* has a brilliant sky which recalls early Corot, whilst the subject and composition are reminiscent of Diaz (though not as strongly as Bazille's other surviving major Fontainebleau landscape).[2] The free, confident brushwork and bright colouring show a strong influence from Monet's more spontaneous technique. The freshness of this relatively large canvas has led recent commentators to speculate if it was all executed on the spot.[3]

The Art Institute of Chicago
(Charles H. and Mary F.S. Worcester Collection)

1. Marandel, Letter 8.
2. *The Forest of Fontainebleau*, Musée d'Orsay, Paris; Daulte, 1952 no. 11.
3. Brettell and Shaefer p. 78.

VIRGILE NARCISSE DIAZ DE LA PENA

[*62] Stormy Landscape

Canvas: 97.8 x 130.5
Studio stamp, lower right.
Lit: Cormack and Robinson no. 19.

This is an unusually bold and dramatic painting by Diaz. The broad brushwork probably places it late in his career, but his works are difficult to date. The treatment of the highlighting in the sky is similar to that found in some of Rousseau's paintings. It is not identifiable with any picture in the Diaz sale Paris, 22-7 January 1877,[1] despite the presence of the sale stamp.

The Syndics of the Fitzwilliam Museum, Cambridge

1. Lugt 37027.

ANTOINE CHINTREUIL

[63] Flowering Broom

Paper on canvas: 54 x 69
Signed, lower right: *Chintreuil*
Lit: De La Fizelière no. 367.

According to the order in De La Fizelière's catalogue, this is a full-size study of 1869 for a painting of the same title.[1] By this time Chintreuil, who had studied with Corot, was relatively well-known and had received a medal at the 1867 Salon. His gentle, naturalistic landscapes were more conservative in their technique

[60]

[63]

than those of the Impressionists. Whilst working at Igny on the river Bièvre just to the south of Paris 1850-57 he had evolved his own type of luminous landscape in which light often breaks dramatically through woodland or across meadows but does not, as in Impressionism, sub-divide into its constituent colours.

Private Collection

1. De La Fizelière no. 366.

VIRGILE NARCISSE DIAZ DE LA PENA

[64] The Forest of Fontainebleau

Canvas: 83.2 x 116.8
Signed and dated, lower right: *N Diaz/70*

By the 1860s Diaz had become well-known for his pictures of the Forest of Fontainebleau. Monet, Renoir, Bazille and Sisley all met him and were influenced by him. His paintings were perhaps the most orthodox of those of the Barbizon masters and depicted the glades and pools that could be found in the Forest. His pictures were never as ambitious or as mannered as Rousseau's. It was probably this straightforward quality which appealed to the Impressionists, though they employed much lighter colours.

Leeds City Art Galleries

Prelude to Impressionism

This section juxtaposes early works by the Impressionists with landscapes by some of their contemporaries and predecessors to whom the term 'Impressionist' would not normally be applied. The complexity and variety of landscapes produced in the 1860s and 70s should not be underestimated. A considerable number of artists were described by critics of the time as having produced 'impressions' rather than rigorous descriptions of nature, and the lack of finish in their work was widely deplored. It was an era of change, variety and – to the regret of conservative, academic critics – confusion as far as landscape was concerned. British readers were apprised of this supposed anarchy in a review of the 1864 Salon which appeared in *The Fine Arts Quarterly Review*: 'In France the most complete eclecticism reigns. For the French landscape painters nature is an object of pure artistic theory. Each has his own system, his own method, his prejudice, to which he submits everything; slothfulness of reproduction is the thing about which they care the least. They aim exclusively at effect, often find it, and do not trouble themselves about the rest.' It is often forgotten that the Impressionists were just a few amongst the thousands of landscape painters working in France from the middle of the century onwards. They had the good fortune to appear when landscape was in a state of flux. The traditional Ecole des Beaux-Arts system of training was increasingly being abandoned and artists could study in the more liberally-run studios of painters such as the Swiss Charles Gleyre (1806-74) which Bazille, Monet, Renoir and Sisley entered in 1862. The rôle of the Salons was challenged, in particular by Courbet with his one-man exhibitions, and on the Normandy coast the tradition of open-air sketching was forcefully revived by Eugène Boudin and his associates.

JEAN-BAPTISTE-CAMILLE COROT

[65] Sèvres-Brimborion, View towards Paris

Canvas: 34 x 49
Signed, lower right: *Corot*
Lit: Robaut no. 1464.

The composition of this painting is indebted to Dutch 17th-century art. The low horizon and centrally receding road with a distant urban view were devices frequently used by landscape painters of that time, most notably by Hobbema in his famous *Avenue at Middleharnis* (National Gallery, London).. Corot's painting, which Robaut dated to 1855-65, shows Paris from the west. It anticipates the frequent use of such a compositional formula by Monet, Pissarro and Sisley, mainly in their works of the early 1870s. Herbert has drawn an instructive contrast[1] between Corot's picture and Sisley's *Louveciennes – the Sèvres Road*[2] of 1873 which shows a similar view of Paris but from nearer to the city. Whereas the Corot, with its figures in traditional costume and its unmade road, is rural and picturesque, the Sisley depicts a suburban scene with trimmed trees and a modern road with drainage and a kerb. The pre-Impressionist picture is general and unspecific, the Impressionist approach is much more exact; its lighting is intended to depict a particular season and time of day.

Musée du Louvre, Paris

1. Herbert, 1982 pp. 140-43.
2. Musée du Louvre, Paris. Daulte, 1959 no. 102.

GUSTAVE COURBET

[66] Scene on the Normandy Coast

Canvas: 42 x 64
Signed, lower left: *G. Courbet*
Lit: Fernier no. 256; Toussaint, 1977/8, no. 2.

Toussaint has associated this painting with Courbet's first visit to the Normandy coast in 1841 and dated it no later than 1842-3; whereas Fernier has dated it 1859 (when Courbet met Boudin at the Saint-Siméon farm at Honfleur). It is difficult to reconcile the confident manner in which Courbet has depicted the sea and sky with some of his rather crude work of the early 1840s.

Musée des Beaux-Arts, Lille

JOHAN BARTHOLD JONGKIND

[67] Notre-Dame seen from the Quai de la Tournelle

Canvas: 27 x 40.5
Signed and dated, lower left: *Jongkind 52*

This particular view of Notre-Dame, from the Left Bank looking north-west, was one that Jongkind depicted on a number of occasions during his career[1] (cf. no. 68). A drawing dated 26 September 1848 is related to this painting.[2] This was an area of Paris that attracted

[65]

[67]

[68]

Jongkind's attention soon after his arrival in 1846. In 1851 he painted a small canvas looking the other way along the Seine towards the newly completed Bridge of La Tournelle.[3] Jongkind's earlier Parisian views, although picturesque and conventional in technique, are important precursors of the Impressionists' urban pictures.

Musée du Petit Palais, Paris.

1. See Cunningham under no. 20.
2. Hefting no. 53.
3. Hefting no. 87.

[68] View of Notre-Dame, Paris

Canvas: 42 x 56
Signed and dated, lower left: *Jongkind 1864*
Lit: Hefting no. 292.

A comparison with the previous picture, showing the same view, reveals many changes in Jongkind's technique in the intervening twelve years. The brushstrokes are now much broader, the finish less smooth; the colour is bolder and the rays of the sun setting behind Notre-Dame are caught reflected on the water's surface. The style of the figures is close to Monet and it was in September 1864 that the two artists worked together at Honfleur. They had first met in 1860.

The Visitors of the Ashmolean Museum, Oxford

STANISLAS-VICTOR-EDOUARD LEPINE

[69] View on the Seine

Canvas: 37 x 60 (sight)
Signed, lower right: *S. Lepine*

This is typical of the many views of the Seine which Lépine executed, one of which he submitted to the First Impressionist exhibition in 1874. His technique was essentially traditional and Corot was the major influence in determining his style. His river views were panoramic and usually taken from the middle of the stream.

Private Collection

CAMILLE PISSARRO

[70] The Donkey Ride at La Roche-Guyon

Canvas: 35 x 51.7
Signed, lower left: *C. Pissarro*
Lit: Pissarro and Venturi no. 45; Lloyd, 1980/1 no. 5; Lloyd, 1984 no. 6.

A political meaning has often been read into this picture due to the obvious contrast between the middle-class trio with the donkeys and the watching peasant children.[1] The general inspiration for this is assumed to have been Courbet's *Young ladies of the village giving alms to a cow-girl in a valley in Ornans*[2] which Pissarro could have seen at the Universal Exhibition in 1855. Apart from Courbet's influence in the subject matter, that of Corot is also discernible in the treatment of the sky and distant trees. The untypical handling of the fields, with their laid-in areas of colour that almost seem to vibrate with light, anticipates Degas's treatment of fields in his various horse-racing pictures. La Roche-Guyon[3] is a small town on the banks of the Seine, approximately half-way between Paris and Rouen. Pissarro is known to have been there in 1865, the probable date of this picture, and had previously visited it each summer 1857-59. Pissarro's view shows, on the far left, a steep chalk escarpment on the north bank of the Seine. The town of La Roche-Guyon lies beyond the trees in the centre of the composition.

Mr and Mrs Tim Rice

1. Lloyd, 1984 identifies the figures as, 'two middle-class women and a boy taking rides on donkeys provided by the two peasant children'. The seated female figure, however, appears to be in her teens and the group more probably consists of a mother with her two children.
2. Metropolitan Museum of Art, New York; Fernier no. 127.
3. See Lloyd, 1985.

CHARLES-FRANCOIS DAUBIGNY

[71] 'Taliferme in Brittany'

Canvas: 84 x 146.5
Studio stamp, lower left
Lit: Hellebranth no. 577; Miles and Spencer-Longhurst p. 10.

Daubigny's visits to Brittany, apart from that of 1867,[1] are not well documented. The dates of his Brittany pictures range from 1855 to 1872. In the 1878 Daubigny sale catalogue, reprinted by Hellebranth,[2] this work is assigned a date of 1865 and is given the title *Taliferme*.[3] The bleak coastal scenery of Brittany evoked a strong response from Daubigny, as it would later from Monet in the 1880s.

The Trustees of the Barber Institute of Fine Arts, the University of Birmingham

1. Moreau-Nélaton, 1925 p. 97.

73. Claude Monet, *Seascape, Shipping by Moonlight*

76. Paul Guigou, *The Banks of the Durance at Puivert (Vaucluse)*

83. Jean-Francois Millet, *Autumn, The Haystacks*

[72]

2. pp. 346-9, Hôtel Drouot, 6-8 May 1878 (Lugt 38360, Hellebranth does not include the drawings section).
3. No. 71 would have been no. 164 in the sale, *Taliferme* 84 x 145 cms; no. 152, of the previous year, was *Taliferme, Bretagne*, Daubigny probably visited Brittany in 1864. A search of guide-books of Brittany has not located 'Taliferme', it may be a misreading of 'Taille-fer' on Belle-Ile off the Brittany coast.

[72] Shipping on the Thames

Canvas: 83 x 129
Signed and dated, lower right: *Daubigny 1866*
Lit: Hellebranth no. 747.

Daubigny first visited England in 1865 and returned in 1866 when he exhibited two paintings at the Royal Academy. He began his series of views of the Thames that year,[1] concentrating particularly on the river to the east of London. The splendid sense of movement which he captures in these pictures and the freedom of his brushwork anticipate Monet's views of Zaandam in 1871 (no. 91). Daubigny was again in London in 1870-1 to escape the Franco-Prussian War and it was then that he introduced two fellow refugees, Monet and Pissarro, to the dealer Durand-Ruel who had opened a gallery there.

Private Collection

1. Hellenbranth nos. 746-63. *Sailboats on the Thames*, Rijksmuseum H. W. Mesdag, The Hague; Hellebranth no. 754 was no. 25 in the 1886 Edinburgh International Loan Exhibition, lent Daniel Cotter, London.

CLAUDE MONET

[*73] Seascape, Shipping by Moonlight

Canvas: 59.5 x 72.5 cm., 23 x 284 ins.
Lit: Wildenstein no. 71.

This is an unusual subject for Monet.[1] It is an expressive picture painted on a dark, slate-blue ground and its handling is reminiscent of Courbet. It is presumably a work of the imagination and can be compared with the moonlit scenes of the 17th-century Dutch artist Aert van der Neer. Such scenes had also been depicted in the 1850s by Monet's friend Jongkind.[2] Wildenstein has dated the picture ca. 1866[3] and identified the port as Honfleur, in which case the view would be to the east across the Seine estuary towards Le Havre. It is painted over an earlier composition, a still-life with a jug.

The National Galleries of Scotland

1. An observation made by Pickvance, 1980.
2. For example Jongkind's *Moonlight on the canal* 1856, Baltimore Museum of Art, Maryland; Hefting no. 155.
3. An inscription on the stretcher in a later hand reads: *Claude Monet 1864*.

[74]

FREDERIC BAZILLE

[74] Aigues-Mortes

Canvas: 46 x 55
Inscribed and signed, lower right: *a M. Fioupiou, son ami
F. Bazille*
Lit: Daulte, 1952 no. 25; Marandel no. 22.

This picture was painted in the summer of 1867 and
shows the walls of the medieval city of Aigues-Mortes,
near Montpellier, from the south. It is one of three
paintings Bazille executed at Aigues-Mortes (no. 75).
The lessons learned while painting with Monet in the
Forest of Fontainebleau in 1865 (no. 61) are evident in
the confident handling of the stagnant marshland. The
dedicatee of this painting, Joseph Fioupiou, a native of
Toulon, was a close friend of Bazille and Degas (with
whom he dined once a week). He was assistant head of
the Exchequer and a collector of prints and drawings.

Musée Fabre, Montpellier

[*75] Gate at Aigues-Mortes

Canvas: 81 x 104
Signed and dated, lower right: *F. Bazille 1867*
Lit: Daulte, 1952 no. 23; Marandel no. 21.

Of the three paintings Bazille executed of the medieval
fortifications of Aigues-Mortes this was the only one of a
particular aspect, the so-called *Porte de la Reine*, the
other two were panoramic views (no. 74).[1] There are
several figure studies for this painting in the Louvre.[2]
The handling of the two figures to the left recalls Monet.
The light effect which Bazille attempts is unusually
ambitious. The sun is hidden by the city walls but a shaft
of light shines through the archway of the gate onto the
dark foreground.

Private Collection, New York

1. The third painting, not included in this exhibition, is Daulte, 1952
no. 24.
2. Sketchbook RF 5259, Marandel p. 223 fig. 23, p. 225 fig. 47.

[77]

PAUL GUIGOU

[*76] The Banks of the Durance at Puivert (Vaucluse)

Canvas: 54 x 80
Signed and dated, lower right: *Paul Guigou. 67*

Like Bazille and Cézanne, Guigou was from the south of France and also knew and mixed with the young Impressionists in Paris. From 1868 he is known to have attended Manet's gatherings at the Café Guerbois, where he was particularly friendly with Monet, Pissarro and Sisley and the writers Burty and Duret. In an article on Guigou, Duret effectively captured the spirit of his paintings: 'His work gives it [Provence] a dusty appearance, the foliage dried out by the sun, the atmosphere limpid, the sky empty or strewn with white clouds. The salient features of Provence are fully reproduced, the sparseness of the terrain, the aridity of the denuded hills, the harshness of the rocky mountains'.[1] Although he painted views of the environs of Paris and at Fontainebleau, the majority of Guigou's pictures were of his native Provence. Many of them, like this example, show the scenery along the river Durance in the Vaucluse mountains to the north of Marseilles. Despite his years in Paris, Guigou's art remained essentially southern and highly distinctive.

Artemis Group and William Beadleston Inc.

1. Duret p. 98.

EUGENE BOUDIN

[77] The Pier at Trouville

Canvas: 64.8 x 92.8
Signed and dated, lower left: *Eugene Boudin-69*; and inscribed lower right: *Trouville.*
Lit: Schmit no. 492.

Many of Boudin's atmospheric paintings of the Normandy coast depict affluent holidaymakers on the beaches there. In this picture he has shifted his attention away from the beach to windblown visitors watching large fishing-boats beating out to sea in squally weather. Boudin's Normandy pictures inspired Monet to paint there. This is the last of a sequence of three major paintings by Boudin of people on piers, the other two having been exhibited at the 1867 and 1868 Salons.[1] The earliest of the three may have suggested to Monet the subject of his similarly windswept painting, *The Pier at Le Havre*, which he successfully submitted to the 1868 Salon.[2] The fashionable world of the Normandy resorts of Trouville, and its offspring Deauville, was often painted by Boudin in the 1860s. An English writer, Henry Blackburn, described Trouville as 'the gayest of the gay ... the world of fashion and delight has made its summer home ... It is a pretty, graceful, and rational idea, no doubt, to combine the ball-room with the sanatorium, and the opera with any amount of ozone'.[3] Boudin first went to Trouville on the advice of Isabey and there is no doubt he felt genuine sympathy for the middle-classes he depicted there, 'but, between you and me, the bourgeois, walking along the jetty towards the sunset, has just as much right to be caught on the canvas, *to be brought to the light'*.[4] His feelings for Trouville fluctuated, however, especially for its richer visitors. In 1867, after a trip to the wilder scenery of Brittany, he found Trouville by comparison, 'a frightful masquerade' and its inhabitants, 'idle poseurs'.[5]

The Burrell Collection,
Glasgow Museums and Art Galleries

1. Ordrupgardsamling and Private Collection; Schmit nos. 407, 436; both were exhibited at the Salon with the title *The Pier at Le Havre* but show the same pier as no. 77 which is certainly of Trouville. This type of subject had first been developed by English artists, notably by Turner and Cox in their pictures of Calais Pier.
2. Private Collection, Wildenstein no. 109.
3. Blackburn p. 53.
4. Jean-Aubry p. 72.
5. Letter to Martin, 28 August 1867, Jean-Aubry p. 65.

GUSTAVE COURBET

[78] The Sea-Arch at Etretat

Canvas: 76.2 x 123.1
Signed, lower left: *G. Courbet*
Lit: Fernier no. 719; Miles and Spencer-Longhurst p. 9.

In August and September 1869 Courbet painted a series of pictures of Etretat on the Normandy coast including *The Cliff at Etretat after the Storm*[1] which was well received at the 1870 Salon. The view here is of the west end of the bay and shows, across the shingle beach, the famous *Porte d'Aval* and the needle beyond. The cliffs on that part of the 'Alabaster Coast', with their striking rock formations caused by the erosion of the sea, had attracted artists since the beginning of the century, including Delacroix and Isabey.[2] Courbet may also have been reminded of the rocky scenery of his native Jura. By the time he left Etretat he had already sold five of his seascapes for a total of 4,500 francs. His paintings at Etretat fall into two general groups; those of storm-tossed waves, and those of the beach which is usually depicted after a storm. Courbet's paintings are essentially romantic in concept and intended to create an emotional response to nature. They ignore the fact that in July and August 1869 the beach at Etretat would have been covered with holidaymakers, as Henry James complained in 1876.[3] A fishing boat is shown in the right of the picture, but in 1860 Jules Michelet had already lamented the decline of the traditional source of income of the village: 'The fish have fled. Etretat is languishing, dying beside a languishing Dieppe ... the contact with Paris, worldly Paris, is the scourge of the region'.[4] Monet's later series of paintings of Etretat, dating from 1883 to 1886, were partly inspired by those of Courbet.[5]

The Trustees of the Barber Institute of Fine Arts,
the University of Birmingham

1. Musée du Louvre, Paris; Fernier no. 745.
2. See Lindon on artists at Etretat.
3. James 'A French Watering Place', letter to the *New York Tribune* 26 August, 1876, quoted in Grad and Riggs p. 239.
4. J. Michelet *La Mer*, Paris, 1983 ed. p. 320, quoted in Brettell and Shaefer pp. 274-5.
5. See his letter to Alice Hoschedé, 1 February 1883, 'I am reckoning on doing a large canvas of the rock at Etretat, although it is terribly audacious on my part to do this after Courbet has done it so admirably, but I shall endeavour to do it differently,...' Wildenstein II p. 223, Letter 312. Monet met Courbet at Etretat in 1869.

[78]

[79] View of Ornans with the Bell-Tower

Canvas: 50.5 x 61
Signed, lower left: *G. Courbet*
Lit: Fernier no. 803; Bowness and Toussaint, 1977/8 no. 56.

Dated by Bowness ca. 1856-9 and by Fernier 1871-2. The observation of light playing over the landscape in this painting is unusually acute for Courbet. Comparison with Sisley's *The Bell-Tower at Noisy-le-Roi: Autumn* of 1874 (no. 103) demonstrates how Courbet's technique remained essentially different from the mature works of the Impressionists. Courbet's landscapes are modelled with the palette knife, the colour range is limited and the contrast between light and dark is uncompromising. The Impressionists saw light in shadow and used a much brighter and more varied palette. The view is from the right bank of the river Loue looking south. A photograph of the same scene taken by Alfred Daber in 1949 reveals how little it has changed since Courbet's day.[1]

Private Collection

1. Mack, pls. 31-2.

EDOUARD MANET

[80] Landscape with a Village Church

Canvas: 30 x 44
Signed, lower right: *Manet*
Lit: Tabarant no. 178.

This painting is similar to a number of small seascape studies executed by Manet in March 1871 at Arcachon, a town on the Bay of Biscay about thirty miles south-west of Bordeaux. Manet took his family there from Oloron-Sainte-Marie, near the Pyrenees, where they had sought refuge in 1870 from the Franco-Prussian War. This may be a sketch of a village near Arcachon. Although the heightened colour which Manet introduced into his pictures in the 1860s was of importance for the development of Impressionism, his brushwork was often smoother and more blended than the loose, open technique of the Impressionists. The Impressionists' concentration on painting out-of-doors was also at odds with much of Manet's essentially studio-based art.

The Visitors of the Ashmolean Museum, Oxford

CHARLES-FRANCOIS DAUBIGNY

[81] Villerville

Panel: 20.2 x 52.8
Signed, lower right: *Daubigny*
Lit: Hellebranth no. 608.

Villerville, on the Normandy coast was, from the late 1850s onwards, one of Daubigny's favourite locations. His most important representation of it was the large canvas included in the 1864 Salon[1] which was allegedly painted entirely on the spot and then reworked in 1872, the probable date of this little painting.

Private Collection

1. Rijksmuseum H. W. Mesdag, The Hague; Hellebranth no. 607.

[82] Apple Blossoms

Canvas: 58.7 x 84.8
Signed and dated, lower right: *Daubigny 1873*
Lit: Sterling and Salinger p. 99; Hellebranth no. 972.

Daubigny had first painted trees in blossom in his 1857 Salon piece *Spring*.[1] It was a popular subject with landscape painters including those of the Impressionist circle, and was treated by Monet in two paintings, also of 1873, of apple trees in blossom.[2]

The Metropolitan Museum of Art, New York
(*Bequest of Collis P. Huntington, 1900*)

1. Musée du Louvre, Paris; Hellebranth no. 957.
2. Metropolitan Museum of Art, New York and Private Collection; Wildenstein nos. 271-2.

JEAN-FRANCOIS MILLET

[*83] Autumn, The Haystacks

Canvas: 85 x 110
Signed, lower right: *J. F. Millet*
Lit: Sterling and Salinger pp. 93-4; Herbert, 1976 no. 149.

In early 1868 Frédéric Hartmann, a wealthy industrialist and formerly a major patron of Théodore Rousseau, commissioned a series of the four *Seasons*[1] from Millet. The cycle had been agreed upon by 26 March, Hartmann's enthusiasm having been fired by a Millet pastel he had seen in Paris. The paintings were based on a group of pastels[2] that had been individually designed for Emile Gavet. Work on the four paintings progressed slowly. They were worked on intermittently, mainly in 1873 and 1874, and *Summer* and *Winter* were never finished. Three of them are the same size, *Winter* is smaller. Some confusion arises out of a request by Millet in a letter of 17 April 1868 for four canvases of which three should have dark, pinkish-lilac grounds and the other a ground of yellow ochre[3] – in fact, both *Summer* and *Winter* have yellow ochre grounds.[4] *Autumn* has a lilac ground which Millet deliberately allowed to show through – even in such a finished, signed and dated picture. This was a practice that was common to the Impressionists as well. The *Seasons* were an epic celebration of man in the landscape. In *Summer* the buckwheat is harvested, in *Winter* the faggot-gatherers bear their burdens homeward, *Spring* and *Autumn* are shown as the seasons of change. In *Spring* the storm-clouds over an orchard are just beginning to clear away; in *Autumn* they are gathering again behind the haystacks in symbolic opposition to the yellow light of late summer which still plays upon the foreground landscape. The true heir of such threatening drama in nature was Van Gogh, who often copied Millet's work.

Metropolitan Museum of Art, New York
(Bequest of Lillian S. Timken, 1959)

1. *Spring*, Musée du Louvre, Paris; Herbert, 1976 no. 147; *Summer, the Buckwheat Harvest*, Museum of Fine Arts, Boston; Herbert, 1976 no. 148; *Winter, Faggot Gatherers* National Museum of Wales, Cardiff, Herbert; 1976 no. 150.
2. That for *Autumn* is in the Rijksmuseum H. W. Mesdag, The Hague; Herbert, 1976 no. 118.
3. Moreau-Nélaton, 1921, III p. 40.
4. Callen, 1982 pp. 68-71.

Impressionism

The Impressionists killed many things, among others the exhibition picture and the exhibition system. The directness of their method and the clearness of their thought enabled them to say what they had to say on a small surface.

WALTER RICHARD SICKERT, 1910

The final part of the exhibition consists of Impressionist landscapes from the late 1860s up to the date of the First Impressionist exhibition in 1874. The Impressionist manner of portraying landscape did not rely on received opinion but on the individual's perception of the optical 'sensations' of colour and light in nature. It was the achievement of the Impressionists to apply to their finished pictures the qualities of freshness of observation and boldness of execution which had previously only been thought suitable for preparatory sketches. The apparent unity of style found in the works of Monet, Pissarro and Sisley in the late 1860s and 70s arose from shared interests in technique and subject-matter – particularly the combination of urban and rural imagery that could be found in the towns and villages around Paris where the Impressionists settled during this period. Argenteuil, Pontoise and Louveciennes were all within easy travelling distance of Paris, but they also had individual characteristics. Equally, the Impressionists themselves had pronounced artistic personalities, as was perceived by some contemporary critics. Thus, Armand Silvestre, in an essay of 1873, described Monet as 'facile and daring', Pissarro as 'realistic and naive' and Sisley as 'harmonious and timid'. It was this very individuality that would later lead to the break-up of Impressionism. Just as the Impressionists had seceded from the Salons, so they also gradually drifted away from their own group exhibitions and only Pissarro contributed to all eight, the last of which was held in 1886.

CLAUDE MONET

[*84] Quai du Louvre, Paris

Canvas: 65 x 92
Signed, lower right: *Claude Monet*
Lit: Wildenstein no. 83.

In April 1867 Monet sought, and was granted, official permission to paint views of Paris from the Louvre.[1] This is one of three resulting pictures, the other two being the *Garden of the Infanta* and *St-Germain l'Auxerrois*.[2] All of them are avowedly modern and unpicturesque in their treatment of the topography of Paris and inclusion of contemporary detail. The *Quai du Louvre* and the *Garden of the Infanta* were painted on canvases of approximately equal size, the former arranged horizontally (the traditional format for a landscape) the latter vertically. They both show the same view and were probably executed largely in the open air. In their precise observation of light and season and with the figures cut off at the edges of the compositions, they have an instantaneity that invites comparison with contemporary photography. In both paintings the view is to the south-east, looking across the Seine from the upper colonnade at the east front of the Louvre towards the Latin quarter, dominated by the dome of the Panthéon in the centre.[3] The avenue of trees in the foreground had been recently planted. In his detailed discussion of Monet's three views from the Louvre, Isaacson[4] placed the *Quai du Louvre* as the first in the sequence and the *Garden of the Infanta* as the third, probably painted about a month later. Monet would develop the idea of the 'series' of paintings devoted to one subject more fully later in his career, particularly with his pictures of 'Rouen Cathedral' and of the 'Haystacks'.

Gemeentemuseum, The Hague

1. Letter, 27 April 1867, to Count de Nieuwerkerke, Wildenstein I p. 448.
2. Allen Memorial Art Museum, Oberlin and Nationalgalerie, Berlin; Wildenstein nos. 85, 84.
3. Left to right in no. 84 one sees the Pont-Neuf, the western end of the Ile de la Cité and the statue of Henri IV; on the left bank the adjacent towers of St-Etienne-du-Mont and Ste-Geneviève; in the centre the dome of the Panthéon and, to the right, that of the Sorbonne.
4. Isaacson, 1966; also Isaacson in Rewald and Weitzenhoffer pp. 16-35.

[85] Huts at Sainte-Adresse

Canvas: 43 x 65
Signed, lower left: *Claude Monet*
Lit: Wildenstein no. 114.

Sainte-Adresse is just to the north-east of Le Havre (of which it is now a suburb) on the Channel coast. In the 1860s it was a fashionable and developing resort, as is demonstrated by Monet's famous painting of 1867 *The Terrace at Sainte-Adresse*.[1] No. 85, which dates from

1867 or 1868,[2] shows the other, more mundane side of life there, the fisherman trudging back to the hut where he keeps his fishing equipment. This concern with a traditional means of livelihood was, on the whole, untypical of Monet. The handling is particularly bold, the touch rapid and broken and the rather sombre green is reminiscent of the paintings of the Barbizon School.

Private Collection, New York

1. Metropolitan Museum of Art, New York; Wildenstein no. 95.
2. Wildenstein states 1868. Monet was also at Sainte-Adresse for several months in 1867.

[*86 *covers*] On the Seine at Bennecourt

Canvas: 81.5 x 100.7
Signed and dated, lower left: *C. Monet/1868*
Lit: Wildenstein no. 110; Brettell and Shaefer no. 47.

In the spring of 1868 Monet stayed, possibly on Zola's recommendation, at the inn at Gloton. His mistress Camille and his young son were also with him. Gloton is a hamlet on the east bank of the Seine, next to the village of Bennecourt. It was an area where Daubigny painted frequently. Cézanne and Zola had also stayed there in 1866.[1] It lies about half-way along the Seine between Paris and Rouen, not far from La Roche-Guyon (no. 70) and Giverny (where Monet settled in 1883). This picture shows Camille seated on the banks of an island in the Seine, *La Grande Ile*, looking across to Gloton. Zola stayed at Bennecourt many times 1866-71 and this image recalls his famous description of Monet in 1868, 'As a true Parisian, he brings Paris to the countryside, he is unable to paint a landscape without placing in it ladies and gentlemen who are all dressed-up'.[2] In the foreground is the rowing-boat in which Monet and Camille had presumably rowed to the island. The river, with its superb reflections (including that of the inn where Monet stayed), acts as a divide between the relatively sophisticated figure of Camille and the traditional scene on the far bank of village women washing clothes in the river. This is one of the most remarkable of all Monet's earlier landscapes; its bold technique and bright colours anticipate his paintings of *La Grenouillère* the following year.

The Art Institute of Chicago (Potter Palmer Collection)

1. Walter, 1962.
2. Zola (1868) p. 111; see also Walter, 1969.

[87] Rowing-boats

Canvas: 33 x 46
Signed, lower right: *Cl.M.*
Lit: Wildenstein no. 137.

This sketch is related to the famous series of pictures of the restaurant on the Seine, *La Grenouillère*, which Monet and Renoir painted when working together in the

84. Claude Monet, *Quai du Louvre, Paris*.

88. Camille Pissarro, *Springtime at Louveciennes*

93. Paul Cézanne, *The Avenue at the Jas de Bouffan*

98. Camille Pissarro, *The Railway Bridge at Pontoise*

99. Alfred Sisley, *The Market Garden*

102. Camille Pissarro, *Kitchen Garden at L'Hermitage, Pontoise*

103. Alfred Sisley, *The Bell-Tower at Noisy-le-Roi: Autumn*

[87]

late summer of 1869.[1] The two rowing-boats do not recur exactly in any of Monet's three paintings of the subject. This would therefore have assumed the function of a discarded study (*étude*) for a more formal, grander composition, and it is as such that Monet's three larger canvases of *La Grenouillère* should be viewed, for he probably intended to submit one of them to the 1870 Salon.[2] The *La Grenouillère* paintings have frequently been cited as signalling the birth of the Impressionist style on account of their broken brushwork and sub-division of colour. As Pickvance[3] and others have pointed out, however, this is an over-simplification. The changes in style of the young Impressionists in the late 1860s and early 70s were not strictly logical and sequential. The choice of subject-matter was certainly innovatory, however, and not to be found in the work of predecessors such as Corot. The *La Grenouillère* series is about contemporary leisure. The restaurant and its bathing area were well-known attractions for day-trippers and weekenders from Paris. *La Grenouillère* was situated at Croissy, on the Ile de la Chaussée on the Seine, between Bougival and Rueil. Bougival, some eleven miles to the west of Paris, was no more than a twenty-minute train journey from the Gare St.-Lazare. Monet had ample opportunity to observe scenes of bourgeois life there, for he was living in the small village of Saint-Michel, near Louveciennes and a little way upstream from Bougival, from late May 1869 until the outbreak of the Franco-Prussian War the following year.

Kunsthalle, Bremen

1. Six in all; those by Monet, Wildenstein nos. 134-36.
2. Formerly Arnhold Collection, Berlin ca. 1909; Wildenstein no. 136, possibly refused by the Salon.
3. Pickvance in Rewald and Weitzenhoffer pp. 38-51.

CAMILLE PISSARRO

[*88] Springtime at Louveciennes

Canvas: 52.5 x 82
Signed, lower right: *C Pissarro*
Lit: Pissarro and Venturi no. 85; Davies pp. 111-2; Lloyd, 1984 no. 12.

Pissarro moved from Pontoise to Louveciennes in 1869, possibly in May, and this was probably executed shortly afterwards.[1] Louveciennes, near Bougival, was one of the small towns and villages west of Paris which were frequently painted by the Impressionists in the late 1860s and early 1870s. The view is away from Louveciennes itself, along the route de la Princesse, towards the houses of Voisins and the Marly aqueduct. It shows a beautiful spring day with a light wind and blossom at the roadside. Scattered houses mark the rising and falling landscape in a manner that recalls Corot's earlier paintings of Ville d'Avray. The picturesque roadway and female figure are also reminiscent of Corot's views of the Sèvres-Brimborion road (no. 65), and Pissarro's debt to the older artist is further emphasised

73

by some of the brushwork and colouring on the shadowed grass verge to the left. Brettell has aptly drawn comparison between this view of Louveciennes by Pissarro and a description of Louveciennes by Victorein Sardou in an essay on the environs of Paris included in a guidebook published in connection with the Universal Exhibition in 1867; 'on one side, grape arbors; on the other, a hollow abounding in greenery; in front houses lost in the foliage … and, crowning it all, the beautiful arcades of the aqueduct, which gives the landscape a grand, Italian air. In sum, the most wonderful arrival in the country that one can find!'[2]

The National Gallery, London

1. Brettell in Lloyd, 1984 p. 15 dates it to the spring of 1869.
2. *Paris Guide par les principaux écrivains et artistes de la France,* Paris, 1867 pp. 1456-7, quoted in Brettell and Shaefer p. 82.

PIERRE-AUGUSTE RENOIR

[89] The Promenade

Canvas: 80 x 64
Signed and dated, lower left: *A. Renoir 70*
Lit: Daulte, 1971 no. 55; House and Distel no. 16.

The beautiful colouring of this painting is indebted to the discoveries concerning light and colour made by Renoir whilst working with Monet at *La Grenouillère* the previous year. The figures are perfectly integrated in the landscape; their white clothing picks up the reflected colours of the areas immediately surrounding them. The subject and pose recall 18th-century rococo art, in particular the *fête galante* and the work of Watteau.

British Rail Pension Fund Works of Art Collection

CLAUDE MONET

[90] Boats in the Pool of London

Canvas: 47 x 72
Signed and inscribed, lower left: *Claude Monet, London*
Lit: Wildenstein no. 167.

This is one of Monet's five surviving pictures from his first visit to London in 1870-1 where he lived during the Franco-Prussian War. This small group consists of two park scenes, the famous *Thames at Westminster* now in the National Gallery, London, and two views of the Pool of London.[1] The reasons for Monet's apparently limited output at this time are not known. Some works may have been destroyed or lost, or Monet may have felt inclined to paint during what would undoubtedly have been an uncertain and disturbing period. The infamous pollution of London's air may have inspired his particular interest in river scenery and encouraged him to study the light and atmosphere there. Various passages, particularly the boat being rowed on the left,

point forward in their semi-abstract treatment to the celebrated *Impression: Sunrise*[2] of 1873 which was another port scene (Le Havre). No. 90 is also a detailed study of work, with lighters bringing goods to the quayside at low tide. It was bought from Monet in 1873 by the collector Albert Hecht, who also owned Corot's *Souvenir des environs du Lac de Nemi* (no. 13).

The Lefevre Gallery, London

1. Wildenstein nos. 164-8.
2. Musée Marmottan, Paris; Wildenstein no. 263.

[91] The Outer Harbour at Zaandam

Canvas: 39 x 71
Studio stamp, lower right
Lit: Wildenstein no. 175.

Monet took his family from England to Holland in the late spring of 1871, finally returning to France via Belgium in the early winter. He stayed in Zaandam, a small town a few miles to the north-west of Amsterdam. Only three letters by Monet from Zaandam survive but he obviously liked the place and the people. The family lodged at the Hôtel de Beurs and his wife Camille gave French lessons. The idea of visiting Holland may have been suggested to him by Daubigny, who was there frequently during 1871-2, or possibly by Jongkind. At that time Zaandam was being industrialised. It still possessed, however, the windmills and bright green houses for which it was famous. Monet's paintings there fall into two main categories: those of the picturesque houses, and his more atmospheric studies of the shipping and the windmills. No. 91 belongs to the latter group and is particularly notable for its economy of means, the sea and sky being almost monochrome and executed in thinned paint. As a study of weather it recalls Boudin; it can also be compared to Daubigny's paintings of shipping on the Thames (no. 72). The view in Monet's picture is towards the south-west and shows the outer harbour at Zaandam, downstream of the Dam, where the river opened out and surrounded a large island. Monet probably took all except one of his Dutch canvases back with him to France.

Private Collection

CAMILLE PISSARRO

[92] The Rue de Voisins, Louveciennes

Canvas: 46 x 55.5
Signed and dated, lower left: *C. Pissarro 1871*
Lit: Lloyd, 1984 no. 16.

In June 1871, after the Franco-Prussian War, Pissarro returned to Louveciennes from England. No. 92 must have been painted in the late autumn of 1871 to judge

[91]

[92]

from the sparse foliage, brown leaves and wintry light. It shows the view down the rue de Voisins, a street which was also painted by Renoir and Sisley. It was one of the earliest Impressionist pictures to enter a British collection as it was probably purchased from Durand-Ruel's summer exhibition in London in 1872 by Samuel Barlow of Stakehill near Middleton, Lancashire.[1]

City Art Gallery, Manchester

1. See Gould. Barlow was Mayor of Middleton and President of the Manchester Arts Club. He owned four Pissarros. It has been suggested that Barlow's interest in Pissarro was stimulated by his friend the German artist William Rathjens (1842-82) who knew Pissarro.

PAUL CEZANNE

[*93] The Avenue at the Jas de Bouffan

Canvas: 38 x 46
Lit: Venturi no. 47; Alley pp. 103-4.

The Jas de Bouffan was an estate on the outskirts of Aix which boasted a fine 17th-century house which belonged to the Cézanne family from 1855 until 1899, when the artist sold it. This is the earliest of his long series of paintings of the avenue of chestnut trees there. This type of motif had appealed particularly to the masters of Barbizon and had already attracted the attention of some of the Impressionists (no. 60). The uncertainty concerning the date of this picture derives from the difficulty in reconciling the fat, juicy application of paint, which indicates the late 1860s or early 70s, with the relatively advanced composition, the discipline of which points to the mid-70s.[1] Compounding the problem is the fact that, as far as is known, Cézanne was in the north of France 1871-4 (Paris, then at Pontoise with Pissaro 1872-4), which is the period into which this painting would fit most easily on grounds of style. It is, of course, possible that Cézanne made an undocumented visit to Aix during these years.

The Tate Gallery, London

1. Opinions have ranged from 1867 to 1875, these are listed by Alley.

CLAUDE MONET

[94] The Petit Bras (small branch) of the Seine at Argenteuil

Canvas: 53 x 73
Signed, lower right: *Claude Monet*
Lit: Wildenstein no. 196.

Argenteuil is situated on the Seine, to the north-west of Paris, a short distance downstream from Saint-Denis. Monet went to live there in December 1871, probably on the advice of Manet, and remained until 1878.[1]

Argenteuil had expanded rapidly since a railway link with Paris had been established in 1851, the journey taking a mere fifteen minutes. The town and its surroundings offered Monet a wide variety of scenery, a meeting-place of the urban and the rural. He concentrates on the latter in this painting. His viewpoint is from the left bank of the river, looking west across the Petit Bras to the Ile Marante, beyond which flows the main stream of the Seine.[2] It is a quiet scene, in spirit and composition akin to the river scenes of Daubigny, but executed very much in an Impressionist technique. The foliage and lighting indicate winter, probably early in 1872, a year in which Monet executed a number of views of the Petit Bras.[3]

The National Gallery, London

1. See Tucker, 1982.
2. To the south was the Plain of Colombes (no. 38).
3. Tucker, 1982 pp. 92-7 for a discussion of Monet's paintings of the Petit Bras.

ALFRED SISLEY

[95] The High Street at Argenteuil

Canvas: 65.8 x 46.7
Signed, lower left: *Sisley*
Lit: Daulte, 1959 no. 269; Lloyd, 1985 no. 6.

Argenteuil is particularly associated with Monet. Sisley stayed there with him in 1872 and others who worked in Argenteuil included Renoir in 1873 and 1874, and Manet in 1874. This painting was correctly identified by Lloyd as a view of the high street (now the rue P. Vaillant-Couturier). Daulte had previously entitled the painting *Rue de Sèvres* in Sèvres and dated it ca. 1877. The church at the end of the street is that of Notre-Dame. A similar view of the high street at Argenteuil was painted by Monet in 1874.[1]

Norfolk Museums Service, Norwich Castle Museum

1. Wildenstein no. 344.

CAMILLE PISSARRO

[96] Landscape at Pontoise

Canvas: 46 x 55
Signed and dated, lower left: *C. Pissarro. 1872*
Lit: Pissarro and Venturi p. 102.

In 1872 Pissarro returned to the Pontoise area on the Oise to the north-west of Paris. He was joined for a while by Cézanne and remained there until 1882. He produced over 300 paintings of Pontoise and its surroundings. This was the most detailed examination of a particular region by any of the Impressionists. His interest in the agriculture of the area was concentrated on the kitchen gardens on the outskirts of the town (no. 102). Paintings

76

[94]

[97]

of the wheatfields, such as this one of 1872, are less common.

The Visitors of the Ashmolean Museum, Oxford

EUGENE BOUDIN

[97] Fishing Boats at Camaret

Canvas: 68.6 x 95.2
Signed and dated, lower left: *E. Boudin-73*
Lit: Schmit no. 894.

Boudin's works are often distinguished by their lively brushwork which at times, however, becomes scratchy and mannered. The controlled technique of this picture bears comparison with the best of Monet's seascapes. Camaret is on the Brittany coast and Boudin visited it regularly in 1870-3. The same group of fishing-boats can be found in his *The Anchorage, Camaret* exhibited at the Salon in 1873.[1]

Private Collection
(on loan to Dundee Art Galleries and Museums)

1. Private Collection; Schmit no. 882.

CAMILLE PISSARRO

[*98] The Railway Bridge at Pontoise

Canvas: 50 x 65
Signed, lower left: *C. Pissarro*
Lit: Pissarro and Venturi no. 234.

Pissarro rarely depicted the railway at Pontoise.[1] This was probably painted in 1873. The iron railway bridge does not play a prominent rôle in the picture and the railway engine is all but obscured by the bridge supports on the opposite banks of the river. By contrast, a number of Monet's paintings of Argenteuil of 1873-4 put much greater emphasis on the railway bridge there. Monet places the bridge at a dramatic angle to the viewer and firmly in the foreground; he emphasises the bridge's size by using a low viewpoint with the spectator looking up towards it with a train steaming across it.[2] Whilst the railway had only an incidental importance for Pissarro at Pontoise, Monet's interest in the subject culminated in his great series of paintings of the Gare St.-Lazare of 1877. The contrasting approaches of Monet and Pissarro to the railway – inescapably symbolic of 'modern life' – reveal a fundamental difference between the two painters at this date. Although by the early 1870s both employed techniques that could justifiably be described as Impressionist, Monet was more aggressively modern in his choice of subject-matter, whilst Pissarro was more attracted to traditional rural scenes. A comparison of this work with Pissarro's *Towpath* (no. 9) of 1864 reveals the changes his painting had undergone in the intervening years, but also demonstrates his enduring fondness for riverside scenery.

Private Collection, Switzerland,
(Courtesy of The Lefevre Gallery, London)

1. Brettell pp. 113-17. The iron bridge was completed in 1863, bringing the railway to Pontoise. The nearest station had previously been at Saint Ouen-l'Aumone on the opposite bank of the Oise. The view is from the Pontoise side of the river.
2. In particular Wildenstein nos. 279, 318-20.

ALFRED SISLEY

[*99] The Market Garden

Canvas: 46 x 61
Signed and dated, lower right: *Sisley. 74*
Lit: Daulte, 1959 no. 138; Lloyd, 1985 no. 10.

Sisley probably executed this picture at or near Louveciennes in the summer of 1874 before his departure for England in July. The sky may have been reworked later.[1] Sisley produced a number of paintings of market gardens in the surrounding areas of Paris in the early 1870s.[2] Pissarro was similarly interested in the agriculture of Pontoise around this date (no. 102). Market gardens had traditionally supplied Paris with fresh fruit and vegetables. The completion of the Paris-Nice railway link in 1870, however, meant that it was possible to transport fresh produce from the south of France to Paris in just twenty-four hours.[3] The market gardens near Paris were increasingly under financial threat from this new competition.

Leeds City Art Galleries

1. Suggested in House no. 107.
2. For example, the incorrectly titled *Cornfield on the hillside, Argenteuil*, Kunsthalle Hamburg; Daulte, 1969 no. 79.
3. Information from Richard Thomson.

[100] Molesey Weir, near Hampton Court

Canvas: 51.5 x 68.9
Signed and dated, lower left: *Sisley 74*
Lit: Daulte, 1959 no. 118; Thompson, C. pp. 20-1.

After the First Impressionist exhibition in 1874, Sisley spent July until October in England at the invitation of the operatic baritone Jean-Baptiste Faure (1830-1914)[1] to whom he had probably been introduced by the dealer Durand-Ruel. After a short time in London he moved to the Hampton Court area and of the pictures which survived from this period, five were chosen by Faure as repayment for financing Sisley's trip.[2] River scenery on the edge of a large city had already been depicted by the Impressionists around Paris and it was a similar environment which Sisley explored around Hampton Court, including the regattas on the Thames. Prior to meeting Durand-Ruel, Faure had collected predominantly Barbizon artists; by 1874, however, he was being ridiculed in the popular press for his patronage of the Impressionists.[3] He had a particular liking for scenes with water such as *Molesey Weir* which shows Sisley using a full Impressionist technique of heightened colour and distinct brushstrokes. Molesey is now much larger than in Sisley's day and is divided into East and West Molesey.

The National Galleries of Scotland

1. On Faure see Callen 1971 and 1974.
2. Daulte, 1959, lists nos. 114-26, to which add *The Inn at Hampton Court*, Bowness and Callen no. 41, and an oil study for Daulte no. 119 (sale Palais Galleria, Paris, 14 June 1967).
3. Faure had begun buying directly from Sisley in 1873, by 1875 he was also a regular collector of Pissarro (see no. 102). Most of his Sisleys were of the 1880s.

[101] View of the Thames and Charing Cross Bridge

Canvas: 33 x 46
Signed and dated, lower left: *Sisley 74*
Lit: Lloyd, 1985 no. 14.

This was painted either during, or as a result of, Sisley's four-month visit to England in 1874 in which he concentrated mainly on views of the River Thames at Hampton Court and Molesey. This view of central London is topographically impossible because St Paul's would not be visible from this viewpoint. Timothy Bathurst[1] has compared this painting to Daubigny's *St Paul's Cathedral seen from the Surrey Bank*[2] of 1873, in which the composition is similar. Daubigny, however, has correctly shown Blackfriars, and not Charing Cross Bridge as Sisley has done. In style and colouring no. 101 bears comparison with Monet's *The Thames and the Houses of Parliament* of 1871.[3]

Private Collection

1. Noted in Lloyd, 1985.
2. National Gallery, London; Hellebranth no. 756.
3. National Gallery, London; Wildenstein no. 166.

CAMILLE PISSARRO

[*102] Kitchen Garden at L'Hermitage, Pontoise

Canvas: 54 x 65
Signed and dated, lower left: *C. Pissarro 1874*
Lit: Pissarro and Venturi no. 267; Brigstocke no. 6.

Pissarro's second period at Pontoise produced some of his finest landscapes in the Impressionist manner.[1] He explored the domesticated landscape around Pontoise in great detail and was particularly interested in the agriculture there. This is an autumn scene of a kitchen garden in the village of L'Hermitage, just to the north-east of Pontoise, where Pissarro lived.[2] Pissarro was described as a rural painter but his ruralism was much less dramatic than the grand, idealised pictures of Breton (no. 5) or Millet. Human activity was less conspicuous in Pissarro's pictures and was more closely integrated into the general view of the landscape. The shape of the terrain around L'Hermitage, with its high horizon and plunging hillsides, was untypical of that found in most Impressionist landscapes. No. 102 was part of the large collection of Impressionist landscapes formed by the singer Faure.[3]

The National Galleries of Scotland

1. The high quality of no. 102 has been revealed by cleaning in 1986.
2. By 1874 L'Hermitage was virtually a suburb of Pontoise as the result of a road-link constructed 1866-8 between the two.
3. Callen, 1971 no. 523. Faure owned over 30 Pissarros, mainly from the 1870s. He also collected Sisley (see no. 100).

ALFRED SISLEY

[*103] The Bell-Tower at Noisy-le-Roi: Autumn

Canvas: 46 x 61
Signed and dated, lower right: *Sisley. 74*
Lit: Daulte, 1959 no. 134; Pickvance, 1971 no. 3.

Sisley was particularly sensitive to seasonal changes in the landscape; he titled this work 'Autumn Morning' (*Matinée d'automne*) when he included it in an 1875 auction.[1] It was probably painted in late October 1874, soon after his return from England. Noisy-le-Roi is a small village near Louveciennes and Marly-le-Roi, west of Paris. Sisley was the most faithful of all the Impressionists to the Louveciennes/Bougival area,[2] returning to work there many times 1870-78.

The Burrell Collection, Glasgow Museums and Art Galleries

1. Vente Morisot, Monet, Renoir et Sisley, Hôtel Drouot, Paris, 24 March 1875 no. 58.
2. See Brettell and Shaefer pp. 79-87.

Artists' Biographies

ACHARD, Jean-Alexis
(Voreppe, Isère 1807-1884 Grenoble)

One of the more important mid-century landscape painters, Achard was the teacher of Harpignies. His paintings of his native Isère and of Grenoble exhibit an attractive combination of classical composition and observation of nature. He moved to Grenoble 1822 where he copied paintings in the Museum and studied under the Lyons painter Dagnan. He travelled to Paris 1830, to Egypt 1835, settled in Paris 1840 and exhibited at the Salon from 1843. Harpignies became his pupil 1846 and they visited the Netherlands 1848-9. Achard lived in Cernay from 1860, returning to Grenoble 1870.

No. 4

ALIGNY, Théodore Caruelle d'
(Château de Chaume, Nièvre 1798-1871 Lyons)

In some respects similar to those of his friend and contemporary Corot, d'Aligny's landscapes were more classical and less varied. He studied in Paris under Watelet and Regnault, first exhibited at the Salon 1822 and shortly afterwards travelled to Italy, where he met Corot 1825, returning to Paris 1827. D'Aligny first worked in the Forest of Fontainebleau 1828, returning frequently thereafter. He was in Italy 1834-5. His State commissions included a journey to Greece 1843-4 to draw the most famous sites there. He was appointed director of the Beaux-Arts de Lyon 1861.

No. 27

BAZILLE, Frédéric
(Montpellier 1841-1870 Beaune-la-Rolande)

Bazille became a close friend of Monet and was one of the most important figures in the early Impressionist circle. His interest in art was stimulated by the Montpellier collection of Alfred Bruyas. Destined by his parents for the medical profession, he moved to Paris in late 1862 and entered Gleyre's studio. He failed his medical exams in 1864 and thereafter devoted himself wholly to painting. In 1865 he shared a studio with Monet, whom he often supported financially. The following year he was accepted at the Salon, but in 1867 drew up a petition for a new Salon des Refusés. He gradually abandoned the open-air Impressionist technique and concentrated on formally composed pictures which depict the scenery of his native south. In the Franco-Prussian War he enlisted in the Zouaves and was killed on active service.

Nos. 41, 61, 74, 75

BERTIN, Jean-Victor
(Paris 1767-1842 Paris)

A pupil of Valenciennes, he was involved in establishing the Rome Prize for historical landscape, many of whose winners trained in his studio – as did Corot briefly in 1822. Bertin first exhibited at the Salon 1793 and was probably in Italy 1806-8. He received State and private patronage under both the Empire and the Restoration.

No. 20

BIDAULD, Jean-Joseph-Xavier
(Carpentras 1758-1846 Montmorency)

A member of the generation of classical landscape painters which included Bertin and Valenciennes, Bidauld's posthumous reputation suffered in the 19th century on account of his membership of the 1836 Salon jury which refused the works of the Barbizon painter Théodore Rousseau – ironically Bidauld had been one of the first artists to work in the Forest of Fontainebleau. Influenced early in his career by Dutch art, he received advice from Vernet in Paris 1783, was in Italy 1785-90 and first exhibited at the Salon 1791. He was the first landscape painter to become a member of the Académie des Beaux-Arts (1823).

No. 19

BONINGTON, Richard Parkes
(Nottingham 1801-1828 London)

Bonington's landscapes in oil and watercolour, praised by his close friend Delacroix, were of crucial importance in introducing the naturalistic English landscape tradition to France. His father was a drawing-master who, in 1817, moved his family to Calais where Bonington was taught by Francia. In 1820 he entered the studio of Baron Gros in Paris. He first exhibited at the Salon 1822 (two watercolours). In England 1825 he met Isabey and Delacroix. The following year he visited Italy, contracting what was probably tuberculosis on the return journey. He made two further visits to England, on the second of which he died.

No. 25

BOUDIN, Eugène
(Honfleur 1824-1898 Deauville)

Boudin's oil-sketches and his exploration of the light and atmosphere of the Normandy coast were of immense importance for the development of Impressionism. He first served as a cabin-boy, then became a stationer and framer in Le Havre where he exhibited works by Millet and Troyon who encouraged him to paint. Awarded a scholarship by the city council, he went to study in Paris 1850 but returned frequently to Le Havre where he met Monet 1858 and advised him to paint out-of-doors. He exhibited at the Salon 1859-97, settled in Honfleur 1860 where he joined the St.-Siméon circle and met Corot. Boudin contributed to the First Impressionist exhibition 1874. His later career included journeys to the Low Countries, the Midi and Venice.

Nos. 7, 34, 77, 97

BRETON, Jules
(Courrières 1827-1906 Paris)

In critical and financial terms, Breton was the most successful French painter of rural life in the 19th century. He studied under de Vigne, Wappers and Drolling, and first exhibited at the Salon 1849. Many of his major pictures were based on observation of village life around his native Courrières, to which he returned to live 1853. Breton was made a Commander of the Legion of Honour 1867. He also wrote poetry, novels and a number of books on painting.

No. 5

CALS, Adolphe-Félix
(Paris 1810-1880 Honfleur)

An attractive minor painter of landscape and genre scenes, Cals trained at the École des Beaux-Arts and in the studio of Cogniet. He first exhibited at the Salon 1831. In 1848 he met the dealer Père Martin and, through him, Corot, Millet, Rousseau and Jongkind amongst others. Martin also introduced him to Count Doria at whose residence, the Château d'Orrouy, he stayed until 1871. Cals met Boudin, Courbet and Monet in the 1860s. At Honfleur he was a regular visitor to the St.-Siméon farm. He participated in the first four Impressionist exhibitions.

No. 38

CASTELNAU, Eugène
(Montpellier 1827-1894 Montpellier)

Castelnau, a close friend of Bazille, was little known until the retrospective exhibition of his work in his native Montpellier (1977). He studied in Paris with the Swiss painter Gleyre and persuaded Bazille to do likewise. He first exhibited at the Salon 1855 but spent most of his life in Montpellier where nearly all of his paintings remain (Musée Fabre and private collections).

No. 40

CEZANNE, Paul
(Aix-en-Provence 1839-1906 Aix-en-Provence)

A boyhood friend of Zola, in 1861 Cézanne abandoned his law studies and went to Paris where he studied painting until 1870. During this period he met Pissarro. Landscapes gradually replaced his early melodramatic subject and figure paintings. His paintings were always rejected at the Salon and he was not accepted there until 1882. Cézanne contributed to the First and Third Impressionists exhibitions, although his objectives became quite different to those of his famous contemporaries. His declared aim was 'to make of Impressionism something solid and durable, like the art of the Museums'.

No. 93

CHINTREUIL, Antoine
(Pont de Vaux, Ain 1814-1873 Septeuil)

Chintreuil's landscapes are particularly notable for their subtle treatment of light. His first job was in a Paris bookshop (in the early 1840s). He was inspired to become a landscape painter by Corot, who influenced him deeply. Chintreuil first exhibited at the Salon 1847. From 1850 (when he met Daubigny) to 1857 he painted at Igny in the Bièvre valley south of Paris with a small community of landscape painters. He moved to La Tournelle Septeuil, near Mantes, 1857 and met Pissarro 1859. He was one of the organisers of the 1863 Salon des Refusés and was on the 1870 Salon jury.

Nos. 42, 57, 63

COROT, Jean-Baptiste-Camille
(Paris 1796-1875 Paris)

Corot was the most versatile and successful French landscape painter of the first half of the 19th century. He studied with the classicising painters Michallon and Bertin and was in Italy 1825-8 where he met d'Aligny and whence he sent works to the 1827 Salon. On his return he worked in many regions of France, especially the Forest of Fontainebleau. There were two further visits to Italy, 1834 and 1843; he also visited Switzerland, Holland and England. He was awarded the Legion of Honour 1846 and became a member of the Salon jury 1848. Although many aspects of his art anticipated Impressionism he remained devoted to the Salon and the ideals it embodied.

Nos. 2, 13, 23, 24, 26, 29, 44, 45, 50, 65

COURBET, Gustave
(Ornans, Franche-Comté 1819-1877 La Tour de Peilz, Switzerland)

Courbet was the most important exponent of Realism in 19th-century French painting and the archetypal Bohemian who remained a controversial figure all his life, both as artist and political activist. His copying of old masters in the Louvre was the most important part of his artistic education which began on his arrival in Paris 1839. He exhibited regularly at the Salon from 1844. *The Stonebreakers* (1849), *A Burial at Ornans* (1850) and *The Painter's Studio* (begun 1854) are among his most famous pictures. Courbet was a great inspiration to the Impressionists, not least for the private exhibitions he organised of his own work in competition with the official Universal Exhibitions of 1855 and 1857. His alleged part in the destruction of the column in the Place Vendôme resulted in his imprisonment and eventual flight from France in 1873.

Nos. 11, 52, 66, 78, 79

DAUBIGNY, Charles-François
(Paris 1817-1878 Paris)

Daubigny, although of an older generation, was particularly sympathetic to the art of the Impressionists. He came from a family of artists and early employment included work as a painter of ornaments and as a restorer. He was in Italy 1836, competed unsuccessfully for the Rome Prize for landscape 1837, and first exhibited at the Salon 1838. In 1840 he studied with Delaroche. He first worked in the Forest of Fontainebleau 1843 and travelled widely in France, painting in Optevoz (east of Lyons), on the Oise north of Paris and on the Channel coast. In 1857 he launched his *botin* (studio-boat) from which he painted river scenery. In the 1850s he was accepted as a major artist, though in the following decade some of his works were criticised for their lack of finish. Acquainted with most of the Impressionists, he encouraged many of them and, in London 1870-1 during the Franco-Prussian War, introduced Monet and Pissarro to the dealer Durand-Ruel.

Nos. 15, 53, 54, 71, 72, 81, 82

DELACROIX, Eugène
(Charenton-Saint-Maurice 1798-1863 Paris)

The leader of the Romantic movement in French painting, Delacroix considered himself primarily a history painter. His interest in landscape, which was stimulated by his close friendship with Bonington, is reflected in the sketches he made on his travels to England 1825, Morocco 1832 and, in France, to Normandy 1843 and the Pyrenees 1845. He also painted landscapes at his country house at Champrosay near Paris, at Nohant and in the Forest of Sénart. His most remarkable landscapes were the oil-sketches and watercolours made on visits to Dieppe 1851-5 which prefigure Impressionism in their bold brushwork and investigation of light and colour.

Nos. 35, 46

DIAZ DE LA PEÑA, Narcisse Virgile
(Bordeaux 1807-1876 Menton)

Diaz was one of the foremost artists of the Barbizon School. Like Renoir, Troyon and other 19th-century painters he trained as a porcelain painter. His earlier pictures of the 1830s and 40s incorporated typical romantic subjects: oriental women, Spanish bathers and nymphs. His first Salon submission 1831 included landscapes which he later developed under the influence of Rousseau (whom he met in the Forest of Fontainebleau 1837). He last exhibited at the Salon 1859. In the 1860s his work influenced Monet, Pissarro, Renoir and Sisley.

Nos. 58, 62, 64

DUBOURG, Louis-Alexandre
(Honfleur 1821-1892 Honfleur)

Dubourg was one of the more successful of the many artists who worked at Honfleur. His best paintings are similar to those of his friend Boudin. He studied under Cogniet in Paris and there met Cals. Appointed to a teaching post at Pont-Audemer, he returned to Honfleur and became a prominent member of the circle of artist centred on the St.-Siméon farm. He exhibited at the Salon 1859-89 landscapes and seascapes of his native region. He founded the Musée d'Honfleur in 1869 (now Musée Eugène Boudin) and was its first curator.

DUNOUY, Alexandre-Hyacinth
(Paris 1757-1841)

Dunouy belonged to the first generation of classical landscapists and studied under Briant. He exhibited at the Salon de la Jeunesse 1781 and at the Salon 1793-1833. He was probably in Italy in the late 1780s and was there again from 1810 under the patronage of Murat, King of Naples. In France he worked in Savoy, Lyons, the Auvergne and Paris and its surroundings. The figures in his paintings were sometimes painted by Demarne and Taunay.

No. 1

GRANET, François-Marius
(Aix-en-Provence 1775-1849 Aix-en-Provence)

A painter of ruins and interiors of churches and monasteries, Granet also left a large collection of landscape sketches, most of which are now in the Musée Granet, Aix, and in the Louvre. He studied under Constantin at Aix where he met Count Auguste de Forbin who later became Director General of French Museums and was instrumental in Granet's appointment to a curatorship in the Louvre, 1826. In 1830, he was charged with the organisation of the Museum of French History which King Louis-Philippe intended to establish at Versailles. In the 1790s Granet had studied in the studio of David. He was in Italy 1802-19 where Ingres executed his famous portrait of him 1807 (Musée Granet). He retired to Malvalat near Aix in 1847.

Nos. 22, 28, 32, 33

GUIGOU, Paul
(Villars-d'Apt 1834-1871 Paris)

Guigou's strong and distinctive art is a mixture of southern and northern traditions of landscape painting. Originally destined for the law by his parents, he received advice and encouragment from Loubon in Marseilles where he exhibited from 1854. He settled in Paris 1860, first exhibiting at the Salon 1863. Around 1868 he became associated with the Café Guerbois circle presided over by Manet. Although he painted in the Ile de France and surrounding areas, his best and most characteristic works were of the south of France, especially the Durance valley.

No. 76

HARPIGNIES, Henri-Joseph
(Valenciennes 1819-1916 Saint-Privé, Yonne)

Harpignies's landscapes owe much to the later style of Corot, whom he met around 1850-1. His works found a steady market throughout his long career. First employed as a commercial traveller, he studied with Achard with whom he visited Brussels 1848. Harpignies was in Italy 1849-52 and 1863-5. He first exhibited at the Salon 1853 and worked in many parts of France, including Fontainebleau, and in 1878 acquired a property in Saint-Privé.

Nos. 47, 48

HERVIER, 'Adolphe'
(Paris 1818-1879 Paris)

Hervier was a minor painter who was sometimes associated with the Barbizon School. His father had trained in David's studio and Hervier himself studied under Cogniet. His work was repeatedly rejected by the Salon jury but he finally gained acceptance 1849. Between 1864 and 1870 he exhibited under his real name, Louis-Henri-Victor-Jules-François.

No. 51

HUET, Paul
(Paris 1803-1869 Paris)

Huet's landscapes belong firmly with Romanticism and he was described as the 'Delacroix of landscape'. He studied in the studios of Guérin and Gros (where he met Bonington 1819). At the Académie Suisse 1822 he met and became a lifelong friend of Delacroix. He was deeply influenced by English landscape painting, in particular by the Constables included in the 1824 Salon. He exhibited at the Salon 1827-69. During his career he travelled widely in France and visited Rome 1842. Perhaps surprisingly, he did not paint in the Forest of Fontainebleau until 1849. Awarded the Legion of Honour 1841, he was chosen to read the funeral oration of his great friend Delacroix in 1863.

No. 8

ISABEY, Eugène
(Paris 1803-1886 Montévrain)

Isabey was a successful painter of seascapes and historical pictures. He forms an important link between the generation of Delacroix and Bonington and pre-Impressionists such as Jongkind, whom he taught. The son of a miniature painter, he exhibited at the Salon 1824-78 and was one of the Court painters of King Louis-Philippe. He visited England 1825, Algeria 1830. Many of his works were based on the scenery of the Normandy coast. In 1844 he met Boudin, who exhibited Isabey's work in his Le Havre shop, and in 1846 Jongkind whilst on a visit to Holland. He maintained a large studio in Paris where he encouraged many younger artists.

No. 6, 55

JONGKIND, Johan Barthold
(Lattrop 1819-1891 La Côte-Saint-André, Isère)

His pre-Impressionist landscapes were of particular importance to Monet, who later in his career acknowledged Boudin and Jongkind as having been the major formative influences on his art. Jongkind trained under Schelfhout at The Hague and travelled to Paris 1846 to study with Isabey. He first exhibited at the Salon 1848. He was in Holland 1855-60 but returned to Paris supported financially by the efforts of Count Doria and the dealer Martin. His paintings were mainly of Paris and of Normandy, where he was a member of the St.-Siméon farm circle and met Monet 1862. He was rejected at the 1873 Salon and ceased to submit works thereafter. He did not participate in any of the Impressionist exhibitions.

Nos. 67, 68

LEPINE, Stanislas-Victor-Edouard
(Caen 1835-1892 Paris)

A minor painter who is best-known for his Parisian views, Lépine participated in the First Impressionist exhibition 1874. He was self-taught but in 1865 received advice from Corot. He also admired Jongkind. Through his dealer Père Martin he enjoyed the patronage of Count Armand Doria but died in poverty. He exhibited at the Salon 1859-89.

No. 69

MANET, Edouard
(Paris 1832-1883 Paris)

As with Cézanne and Courbet, Manet came from an affluent family. He studied in Couture's studio 1850-6, during which period he travelled widely within Europe, much of his time being spent in copying old masters. He first exhibited at the Salon 1861 but was frequently rejected thereafter. His *Déjeuner sur l'Herbe* caused a sensation at the 1863 Salon des Refusés. Manet defies classification. He is not an 'Impressionist' in the sense that he was not primarily concerned with questions of colour and light which were the main preoccupations of the so-called Impressionists. Though friendly with many of them and sharing their ideals, Manet refused to exhibit at any of the Impressionist exhibitions held during his lifetime, preferring instead to triumph at the Salon. Manet is best remembered for his portraits and figures paintings and landscapes are a minor part of his surviving output.

No. 80

MICHALLON, Achille-Etna
(Paris 1796-1822 Paris)

He was the winner of the first Rome Prize for landscape 1817. Michallon's talent was precocious and he exhibited at the Salon 1812 at the age of sixteen. He studied under David and some of the foremost landscape painters – Valenciennes, Dunouy and Bertin. He was at the French Academy in Rome 1817-21, returning to Paris where Corot was his pupil.

No. 21

MICHEL, Georges
(Paris 1763-1843 Paris)

Michel, who abandoned history painting for landscapes, was a prolific artist, being inspired by the 17th-century Dutch masters. He produced many copies of Dutch paintings for dealers and was also employed as a restorer of Netherlandish paintings in the Louvre. Michel exhibited at the Salon 1791-1814 with little success, and died in obscurity. His reputation was revived in the 1870s by an exhibition of his work at the Durand-Ruel Gallery in London in 1872 and by Sensier's 1873 monograph on him. Michel's paintings were widely collected in Britain in the later 19th century.

No. 43

MILLET, Jean-François
(Gruchy 1814-1875 Barbizon)

Millet has gained deserved recognition in this century as the greatest of all painters of peasant scenes. He trained in Cherbourg with Mouchel and Langlois, then in Paris with Delaroche. He first exhibited at the Salon 1840. After moving to Barbizon in 1849 he concentrated on rural scenes to which he gave an epic grandeur. Many, such as *The Gleaners* (1857), attracted controversy and accusations of being politically subversive. He was awarded the Legion of Honour 1868. In his last years he concentrated particularly on landscape and enjoyed international fame.

No. 83

MONET, Claude
(Paris 1840-1926 Giverny)

Monet was undoubtedly the leading figure of early Impressionism. His meeting with Boudin at Le Havre 1858 was more important for his development than any formal training he received either at Le Havre or in Paris to which he moved 1859 and where he first met Pissarro. In 1863 he worked with Bazille, Renoir and Sisley at Chailly in the Forest of Fontainebleau and was strongly influenced by the Barbizon painters. He first exhibited at the Salon 1865. He was in London during the Franco-Prussian War; and then in Holland, 1871. Monet's *Impression: Sunrise* was included in the First Impressionist exhibition and earned the group its derogatory title. For most of the 1870s he lived at Argenteuil. In 1883 he moved to Giverny where he developed his famous water garden. The first of his 'series' pictures, *Haystacks* was begun in 1890, to be followed by the *Poplars*, *Cathedrals* and the London and Venice views. The greatest of these, the *Nymphéas*, was commissioned by Clemenceau and presented to the French State in 1921.

Nos. 73, 84, 85, 86, 87, 90, 91, 94

PISSARRO, Camille
(St Thomas, Virgin Islands 1830-1903 Paris)

Pissarro was one of the major figures of Impressionism and was the only artist to participate in all of the group's eight exhibitions. After early schooling in Paris he returned to the Virgin Islands destined for a career in the family business. In 1852-4 he was in Venezuela with the Danish painter Melbye; the following year he travelled to Paris where he saw the Universal Exhibition and met and was profoundly influenced by Corot. Pissarro first exhibited at the Salon 1859 and also met Monet that year. His two stays in Pontoise (1866-9 and 1872-82) were of great importance to the development of his art. During the Franco-Prussian War 1870-1 he lived at Lower Norwood, London. In 1884 he moved to Eragny-sur-Epte where he remained for the rest of his life. His friendship with Signac in the mid-80s encouraged his interest in Neo-Impressionist colour theory. Pissarro was the most popular of all the Impressionists and was generous in his encouragement and advice to younger artists.

Nos. 9, 10, 12, 39, 59, 70, 88, 92, 96, 98, 102

RENOIR, Pierre-Auguste
(Limoges 1841-1919 Cagnes)

Renoir's are the most decorative of all the Impressionists' paintings. He trained as a porcelain painter, then in 1862 studied at the Ecole des Beaux-Arts and attended Gleyre's studio. That same year he met and was encouraged by Diaz. He first exhibited at the Salon 1864. Landscape played an important rôle in his early work, though he later concentrated increasingly on the female nude. In 1869 he and Monet executed their well-known series of paintings of *La Grenouillère*. During the Franco-Prussian War he served in the 10th Cavalry Regiment. He only participated in the first three Impressionist exhibitions, thereafter preferring to show at the Salon. He was awarded the Legion of Honour 1900 and spent his last years on his estate at Cagnes in the south of France.

No. 89

ROUSSEAU, Philippe
(Paris 1816-1887 Acquigny)

Rousseau was primarily a still-life painter but his early Salon exhibits 1834-41 were all landscapes. He is said to have studied under Gros and Victor Bertin. Rousseau was particularly influenced by the 18th-century masters Chardin and Oudry. His work was popular during the Second Empire and he received many commissions from the court of Napoleon III.

No. 49

ROUSSEAU, Pierre-Etienne-Théodore
(Paris 1812-1867 Barbizon)

The major artist of Barbizon, he first exhibited at the Salon 1831 but was excluded 1836-47, becoming known as *'Le Grand Refusé'*. He trained with a cousin who was a landscape painter and then with Rémond. Rousseau first painted in the Forest of Fontainebleau 1826-9, travelled to the Auvergne 1830 and in the 1840s visited the Landes near Bordeaux and Berry, amongst other regions. From about 1837 he rented a studio in Barbizon nearly every summer and finally settled there. His work gained widespread and belated recognition in the 1850s and 60s. He died in Millet's arms.

Nos. 3, 30, 31, 36, 37

SISLEY, Alfred
(Paris 1839-1899 Moret-sur-Loing)

Sisley is often unjustly overlooked because of his alleged failure to keep pace with later developments in Impressionism. His earlier work is as assured as that of any of the other Impressionists. Born in France of Anglo-French parents, he entered Gleyre's studio 1862 where he met Monet, Renoir and Bazille. All four artists worked in the Forest of Fontainebleau 1863 and 1865. He exhibited at the Salon 1866 and 1870. In 1869 he became a member of the Café Guerbois circle. During the Franco-Prussian War he was at Louveciennes, an area he painted frequently in the 1870s. He participated in the First, Second, Third and Seventh Impressionist exhibitions.

No. 60, 95, 99, 100, 101, 103

TROYON, Constant
(Sèvres 1810-1865 Paris)

Troyon established an international reputation as an animal painter. He came from a family of porcelain painters and initially trained as such (like Diaz, Renoir and others). He first exhibited at the Salon 1833. In 1843 he met Rousseau and Dupré and became associated with the Barbizon School. He was awarded the Legion of Honour 1849 and his works were widely exhibited abroad where he had many followers. In his later years he concentrated more on landscape (particularly of the Channel coast) and gave support and advice to Boudin and Monet.

No. 56

VALENCIENNES, Pierre-Henri de
(Toulouse 1750-1819 Paris)

Valenciennes was an influential teacher and landscape painter. His treatise *Elémens de Perspective Pratique* (1800) became the standard text on academic landscape theory in France and laid particular emphasis on the importance of the preparatory sketch painted out-of-doors. Valenciennes may have been taught oil-sketching by the great marine painter Joseph Vernet whom he met whilst in Rome 1777-84/5. He first exhibited at the Salon 1787. In 1812 he was appointed Professor of Perspective at the Ecole des Beaux-Arts. Valenciennes was instrumental in instituting the Rome Prize for landscape in 1817, in which year he revisited Rome. The majority of his many Italian sketches are now in the Louvre and the Bibliothèque Nationale in Paris.

Nos. 16, 17

Bibliography

Bibliographical references have been kept to a minimum and refer only to catalogues raisonnés and other publications which give fuller details of provenance, literary references and exhibition history. For further information the reader is advised to consult the bibliographies in Brettell and Shaefer, Moffett and Rewald. In addition to the publications cited below the following have been of particular use in the compilation of this catalogue:

Bacou, R. and others *French Landscape Drawings and Sketches*, Catalogue of exhibition at British Museum, London, 1977.

Champa, K. *Studies in Early Impressionism*, New Haven and London, 1973.

Conisbee, P. 'Pre-Romantic *Plein-Air* Painting', *Art History*, 1979, pp. 413-28.

Galassi, P. *Before Photography, Painting and the Invention of Photography*, Catalogue of exhibition at New York/Omaha/Los Angeles/Chicago, 1981.

Harambourg, L. *Dictionnaire des Peintres Paysagistes Français au XIXe Siècle*, Neuchâtel, 1985.

Pillement, G. *Les Pre-Impressionistes*, Zoug, 1974.

Publications cited in essay and catalogue entries

Alley, R. *Catalogue of the Tate Gallery's Collection of Modern Art other than works by British artists*, London, 1981.

Aubrun, M. *Théodore Caruelle d'Aligny et ses compagnons*, Catalogue of exhibition at Orléans/Dunkirk/Rennes, 1979

Baer, J. *A.-F. Cals 1810-1880*, Catalogue of exhibition at Hazlitt, London, 1969.

Baudelaire, C. *Art in Paris 1845-1862, Reviews of Salons and other exhibitions* (translated and edited by J. Mayne), London, 1965.

Baudson, F. *Antoine Chintreuil 1814-1873*, Catalogue of exhibition at Bourg-en-Bresse/Pont-de-Vaux, 1973

Beckett, R. B. 'Constable and France', *The Connoisseur*, 1956, pp. 249-55.

La Bedollière, E. and I. Rousset, *Le Tour de Marne*, Paris, 1865.

Bergeret-Gourbin, A.-M. 'Les bains de mer à Honfleur de Louis-Alexandre Dubourg' *La Revue du Louvre*, 1980, pp. 330-1.

Bergeret-Gourbin, A.-M. *Louis-Alexandre Dubourg 1821-1891*, Catalogue of exhibition at Musée Eugène Boudin, Honfleur, 1985.

Blackburn, H. *Artistic Travel*, London, 1892.

Boime, A. *The Academy and French Painting in the Nineteenth Century*, London, 1971.

Bowness, A. and A. Callen *The Impressionists in London*, Catalogue of exhibition at Hayward Gallery, London, 1973.

Bowness, A. and H. Toussaint *Gustave Courbet 1819-1877*, Catalogue of exhibition, London/Paris, 1977/8.

Brettell, R. *Pissarro and Pontoise: The Painter in a Landscape*, Ph.D. Dissertation, Yale University, 1977, Ann Arbor microfiche, 1978.

Brettell, R. and C. Lloyd *Catalogue of Drawings by Camille Pissarro in the Ashmolean Museum, Oxford*, Oxford, 1980.

Brettell, R. and S. Shaefer *A Day in the Country. Impressionism and the French Landscape*, Catalogue of exhibition at Los Angeles/Chicago/Paris, 1984/5.

Brigstocke, H. *French and Scottish Paintings, The Richmond-Traill Collection*, Catalogue of exhibition at National Gallery of Scotland, Edinburgh, 1980.

Busch, G. *Zurück zur Natur*, Catalogue of exhibition at Kunsthalle, Bremen, 1977/8.

Callen, A. *Jean-Baptiste Faure, 1830-1914*, MA Dissertation, University of Leicester, 1971.

Callen, A. 'Faure and Manet', *Gazette des Beaux-Arts*, LXXXIII, 1974, pp. 157-58.

Callen, A. *Techniques of the Impressionists*, London, 1982.

Castagnary, J. *Salons*, Paris, 1892.

Cormack, M. and D. Robinson *Landscapes from the Fitzwilliam*, Catalogue of exhibition at Hazlitt, Gooden and Fox, London, 1974.

Coutagne, D. *Granet. Paysages de L'Ile de France, Aquarelles et Dessins, Collections du Musée Granet, Aix-en-Provence*, Aix, 1984.

Cunningham, C. *Jongkind and the Pre-Impressionists. Painters of the Ecole Saint-Siméon*, Catalogue of exhibition at Northampton/Williamstown, 1976/7.

Daulte, F. *Frédéric Bazille et son temps*, Geneva, 1952.

Daulte, F. *Alfred Sisley: Catalogue raisonné de l'oeuvre peint*, Lausanne, 1959.

Daulte, F. *Auguste Renoir, Catalogue raisonné de l'oeuvre peint, I. Figures 1860-1890*, Lausanne, 1971.

Davies, M. *National Gallery Catalogues. French School. Early 19th century, Impressionists, Post-Impressionists etc.*, London, 1970.

Dejean, X. *Eugène Castelnau (1827-1894)*, Catalogue of exhibition at Musée Fabre, Montpellier, 1977.

Delacroix, E. *Journal*, three vols., Paris, 1950.

Delvau, A. 'Les Châteaux des Rois de Bohème, La Ferme Saint-Siméon, *Figaro* 1 August 1865.

Deperthes, J. B. *Théorie du Paysage*, Paris, 1818.

Dubuisson, A. and R. Hughes, *Richard Parkes Bonington: his Life and Work* London, 1924.

Duret, T. 'Un grand peintre de La Provence, Paul Guigou,' *L'Art et les Artistes*, no. 87, June, 1912.

Fernier, R. *La vie et l'oeuvre de Gustave Courbet*, two vols., Lausanne/Paris, 1977/8.

Fidell-Beaufort, M. and J. Bailly-Herzberg, *Daubigny*, Paris, 1975.

De La Fizelière, A. and others, *La Vie et l'Oeuvre de Chintreuil*, Paris, 1874.

Fromentin, E. *Les maîtres d'autrefois: Belgique-Hollande*, Paris, 1876.

Gerkens, G. and U. Heiderich *Katalog der Gemälde des 19. und 20. Jahrhunderts in der Kunsthalle Bremen*, two vols., Bremen, 1973.

Gillow, N. *Catalogue of Paintings, City of York Art Gallery, Volume III*, York, 1974.

Gould, C. 'An Early Buyer of French Impressionists in England', *The Burlington Magazine*, 1966, pp. 141-2.

Gowing, L. and P. Conisbee *Painting from Nature*, Catalogue of exhibition, Cambridge/London, 1980/1.

Grad, B. and T. Riggs *Visions of City and Country. Prints and Photographs of Nineteenth-Century France*, Catalogue of exhibition at Worcester Art Museum, 1982.

Green, N. *Théodore Rousseau 1812-1867*, Catalogue of exhibition at Norwich/London, 1982.

Grunchec, P. *Le Grand Prix de Peinture. Les concours des Prix de Rome de 1797 à 1863*, Paris, 1983.

Grunchec, P. *The Grand Prix de Rome. Paintings from the Ecole des Beaux-Arts 1797-1863*, Catalogue of exhibition organised by the International Exhibitions Foundation, Washington, 1984/5.

Gutwirth, S. 'Jean-Victor Bertin un paysagiste néo-classique (1767-1842)', *Gazette des Beaux-Arts*, LXXXIII, 1974, pp. 337-58.

Gutwirth, S. *Jean-Joseph-Xavier Bidauld*, Catalogue of exhibition at Carpentras/Angers/Cherbourg, 1978.

Hefting, V. *Jongkind, sa vie, son oeuvre, son époque*, Paris, 1975.

Hellebranth, R. *Charles-François Daubigny 1817-1878*, Morges, 1976.

Herbert, R. *Barbizon Revisited*, Catalogue of exhibition at San Francisco/Toledo Cleveland/Boston, 1962.

Herbert, R. *Jean-François Millet*, Catalogue of exhibition at London/Paris, 1975/6.

Herbert, R. 'Industry in the changing landscape from Daubigny to Monet', *French Cities in the 19th Century* (ed. J. Merriman), London, 1982, pp. 139-64.

House, J. *Impressionism. Its Masters, its Precursors, and its Influence in Britain*, Catalogue of exhibition at Royal Academy, London, 1974.

House, J. and A. Distel *Renoir*, Catalogue of exhibition at London/Paris/Boston, 1985/6.

Huault-Nesme, L. *Jean Achard. Peintures*, Catalogue of exhibition at Musée de Grenoble, 1984/5.

Isaacson, J. 'Monet's Views of Paris' *Allen Memorial Art Museum Bulletin*, Vol 24, no. 1, 1966 pp. 5-20.

Jacobs, M. *The Good and Simple Life. Artist Colonies in Europe and America*, Oxford, 1985.

Jean-Aubry, G. *Eugène Boudin*, London, 1969.

Johnson, L. *Delacroix*, London, 1963.

Jullien, A. and R. Jullien, 'Les campagnes de Corot au nord de Rome (1826-1827)', *Gazette des Beaux-Arts*, XCIX, 1982, pp. 179-202.

Jullien, A. and R. Jullien 'Corot dans les Montagnes de la Sabine' *Gazette des Beaux-Arts*, CIII, 1984 pp. 179-97.

Lacambre, G. *Les paysages de Pierre-Henri de Valenciennes. Dossier du Département des Peintures, no. 11, Musée du Louvre*, Paris, 1976.

Lanöe, G. and T. Brice *Histoire de l'Ecole Française du Paysage*, Paris, 1907.

Lindon, R. 'Etretat et les peintres', *Gazette des Beaux-Arts*, LI, 1958, pp. 353-60.

Lloyd, C. and others *Camille Pissarro 1830-1903*, Catalogue of exhibition at London/Paris/Boston, 1980/1.

Lloyd, C. *Retrospective Camille Pissarro*, Catalogue of exhibition at Tokyo/Fukuoka/Kyoto, 1984.

Lloyd, C. *Retrospective Alfred Sisley*, Catalogue of exhibition at Tokyo/Fukuoka/Nara, 1985.

Lloyd, C. 'Reflections on La Roche-Guyon and the Impressionists', *Gazette des Beaux-Arts*, CVI, 1985, pp. 37-44.

Lugt, F. *Répertoire des catalogues de ventes, 1861-1900*, Vol III, The Hague, 1964.

McLaren Young, A. and others *The Paintings of James McNeill Whistler*, two vols., New Haven and London, 1980.

Mack, G. *Gustave Courbet*, New York, 1951.

Marandel, J. *Frédéric Bazille and Early Impressionism*, Catalogue of exhibition at Art Institute, Chicago, 1978.

Miles, H. and P. Spencer-Longhurst *Handbook of the Barber Institute of Fine Arts*, Birmingham, 1983.

(Minneapolis) *The Past Rediscovered: French Painting 1800-1900*, Catalogue of exhibition at Minneapolis Institute of Arts, 1969.

Miquel, P. *Paul Huet: de l'aube romantique à l'aube impressioniste*, Sceaux, 1962.

Miquel, P. *Le Paysage Français au XIXe fiècle 1824-1874*, three vols., Maurs-La-Jolie, 1975.

Miquel, P. *Eugène Isabey 1803-1886. La Marine au XIXe siècle* Vols IX, X, Maurs-La-Jolie, 1980.

Moffett, C. and others *The New Painting. Impressionism 1874-1886*, Catalogue of exhibition at San Francisco/Washington, 1986.

Moreau-Nélaton, E. *Millet raconté par lui-même*, three vols., Paris, 1921.

Moreau-Nélaton, E. *Daubigny raconté par lui-même*, Paris, 1925.

Nochlin, L. *Impressionism and Post-Impressionism*, Princeton, 1966.

(Philadelphia) *The Second Empire 1852-1870. Art in France under Napoleon III*, Catalogue of exhibition at Philadelphia/Detroit/Paris, 1978/9.

Pickvance, R. *Alfred Sisley (1839-99). Impressionist Landscapes*, Catalogue of exhibition at Nottingham University, 1971.

Pickvance, R. in 'Current and Forthcoming Exhibitions', *The Burlington Magazine*, 1980, pp. 705-6.

Pissarro, C. *Letters to his son Lucien* (edited with the assistance of Lucien Pissarro by John Rewald), London, 1980.

Pissarro, L. and L. Venturi *Camille Pissarro, son art-son oeuvre*, two vols., Paris, 1939.

Pointon, M. *The Bonington Circle: English Watercolour and Anglo-French Landscape*, Brighton, 1985.

Pontier, A. *Le Musée d'Aix, seconde partie*, Aix, 1900.

Randall, L. *The Diary of George A. Lucas. An American Art Agent in Paris, 1857-1909*, two vols., Princeton, 1979.

Rewald, J. *The History of Impressionism*, New York, 1973.

Rewald, J. and F. Weitzenhoffer (eds.) *Aspects of Monet. A symposium on the artist's life and times*, New York, 1984.

Robaut, A. *L'Oeuvre de Corot; Catalogue raisonné et illustré*, three vols., Paris, 1905.

Robaut, A. and E. Chesnau, *L'oeuvre complet d'Eugène Delacroix*, Paris, 1985.

Roethlisberger, M. *Claude Lorrain: The Paintings*, two vols., London, 1961.

Rosenberg, P. and others *De David à Delacroix, La peinture française de 1774 à 1830*, Catalogue of exhibition at Paris/Detroit/New York, 1974/5.

Schmit, R. *Eugène Boudin, 1824-1898*, three vols., Paris, 1973.

Scrase, D. *The John Tillotson Bequest. Paintings and Drawings of the Barbizon School, Fitzwilliam Museum, Cambridge*, Catalogue of exhibition at Cambridge/London, 1986.

Sérullaz, M. 'Un nouveau Delacroix entre au Louvre: *La mer vue des hauteurs de Dieppe*', *La Revue du Louvre*, 1980, pp. 10-13.

Sillevis, J. and H. Kraan *De School van Barbizon, Franse Meesters van de 19de Eeuw*, Catalogue of exhibition at Ghent/The Hague/Paris, 1985/6.

Silvestre, A. 'Henri Harpignies', *Société d'Aquarellistes Français, Ouvrage d'Art*, 1883, I pp. 132-4.

Spencer, M. *R. P. Bonington 1802-1825*, Catalogue of exhibition at Castle Museum and Art Gallery, Nottingham, 1965.

Sterling, C. and M. Salinger *French Paintings. A Catalogue of the Collection of the Metropolitan Museum of Art, XIX Century*, New York, 1966.

Sturges, H. and others *Jules Breton and the French Rural Tradition*, Catalogue of exhibition at Omaha/Memphis/Williamstown, 1982/3.

Tabarant, A. *Manet et ses oeuvres*, Paris, 1947.

Thompson, C. *The Maitland Gift and related pictures, National Gallery of Scotland*, Edinburgh, 1963.

Thompson, C. and H. Brigstocke, *National Gallery of Scotland. Shorter Catalogue*, Edinburgh, 1978.

Thompson, J. and others *The Peasant in French 19th Century Art*, Catalogue of exhibition at Douglas Hyde Gallery, Dublin, 1980.

Thoré, T. *Salons*, two vols., Paris, 1870.

Toussaint, H. *Le Musée du Luxembourg en 1874*, Catalogue of exhibition at Grand Palais, Paris, 1974.

Toussaint, H. *Hommage à Corot*, Catalogue of exhibition at Musée de l'Orangerie, Paris, 1975.

Tucker, P. *Monet at Argenteuil*, New Haven and London, 1982.

Tucker, P. 'The first Impressionist exhibition and Monet's *Impression, Sunrise*: a tale of timing, commerce and patriotism', *Art History*, 1984 pp. 465-76.

Valenciennes, P. *Elémens de Perspective Pratique*, Paris, 1800.

Venturi, L. *Cézanne: Son Art-son oeuvre*, two vols., Paris, 1936.

Vignon, C. *Exposition Universelle de 1855 Beaux-Arts*, Paris, 1855.

Vollard, A. *Tableaux, Pastels et Dessins de Pierre-Auguste Renoir*, two vols., Paris, 1918.

Walter, R. 'Cézanne à Bennecourt en 1866', *Gazette des Beaux-Arts*, LIX, 1962, pp. 103-18.

Walter, R. 'Critique d'Art et Vérité: Emile Zola en 1868', *Gazette des Beaux-Arts*, LXXIII, 1969, pp. 225-34.

Weisberg, G. 'Vestiges of the Past: The Brittany 'pardons' of late nineteenth-century French painters', *Arts Magazine*, November, 1980, pp. 134-8.

Weisberg, G. *The Realist Tradition. French Painting and Drawing 1830-1900*, Catalogue of exhibition at Cleveland/Booklyn/St. Louis/Glasgow, 1980/2.

Weisberg, G. ed. *The European Realist Tradition*, Bloomington, 1982.

Whitney, W. 'Pierre-Henri Valenciennes: An Unpublished Document', *The Burlington Magazine*, 1976, pp. 225-7.

Wildenstein, D. *Claude Monet, Biographie et catalogue raisonné*, four vols., Lausanne and Paris, 1974-85.

Zola, E. *Le bon combat de Courbet aux Impressionistes. Anthologie d'écrits sur l'art*, Paris, 1974.

List of Lenders

Mr and Mrs Jack Baer 38
British Rail Pension Fund Works of Art Collection 89
Dr Peter Nathan 46
Private Collections 1, 16, 17, 18, 21, 23, 31, 55, 58, 63, 69, 72, 75, 79, 81, 85, 91, 97, 98, 101
Mr and Mrs Tim Rice 59, 70
The Searle Collection 50

Aix-en-Provence, Musée Granet 22, 28, 32, 33
Barnard Castle, Bowes Museum 11
Birmingham, Barber Institute of Fine Arts 71, 78
Bordeaux, Musée des Beaux-Arts 8
Bremen, Kunsthalle 27, 42, 60, 87
Cambridge, Fitzwilliam Museum 10, 20, 29, 30, 37, 39, 47, 62
Chicago, Art Institute 13, 61, 86
Dublin, National Gallery of Ireland 5
Edinburgh, National Galleries of Scotland 12, 15, 25, 44, 48, 56, 73, 100, 102
Ghent, Museum voor Schone Kunsten 45
Glasgow, The Burrell Collection 77, 103
Glasgow, Museum and Art Gallery 3, 9, 51
The Hague, Gemeentemuseum 84
Le Havre, Musée des Beaux-Arts 7, 34
Honfleur, Musée Eugène Boudin 14
Leeds, City Art Galleries 43, 64, 99
Lille, Musée des Beaux-Arts 66
London, Artemis Group and William Beadleston Inc. 76
London, Lefevre Gallery 90
London, National Gallery 49, 88, 94
London, Stoppenbach and Delestre Limited 6, 19
London, Tate Gallery 93
Manchester, City Art Gallery 92
Montpellier, Musée Fabre 40, 41, 52, 74
New York, Metropolitan Museum of Art 53, 82, 83
Norwich, Castle Museum 95
Oxford, Ashmolean Museum 24, 26, 68, 80, 96
Paris, Musée du Louvre 4, 35, 54, 65
Paris, Musée du Petit Palais 67
York, City Art Gallery 36
Zürich, Kunsthaus 2
Zürich, Gallery Bruno Meissner 57

Photographic Credits

Photographie Bulloz 67
A. Cooper Fig. 2
Prudence Cuming Associates Ltd 19
Alain Danvère 8
S. A. Studio Lourmel Fig. 1
Claude O'Sughrue 40, 41, 52, 74
Photorama S.A. 7, 34
Bernard Terlay 33